AmericanHeritage ®
Book of
Great American Speeches for Young People

Edited by Suzanne McIntire

John Wiley & Sons, Inc.
New York • Chichester • Weinheim • Brisbane • Singapore • Toronto

For my children,
Phinney and Will

Published by John Wiley & Sons, Inc.
Published simultaneously in Canada

Design and production by Navta Associates, Inc.

Library of Congress Cataloging-in-Publication Data

American Heritage book of great American speeches for young people / edited by Suzanne McIntire.
    p. cm.
    Includes index.
    ISBN 0-471-38942-0 (acid-free paper)
    1. Speeches, addresses, etc., American—Juvenile literature. [1. Speeches, addresses, etc. 2. United States—History—Sources.] I. Title: Book of great American speeches for young people. II. McIntire, Suzanne, 1951–

PS662 .A44   2001
815.008—dc21
                                 00-043749

Printed in the United States of America

10 9 8 7 6 5 4 3 2 1

Acknowledgments

It has been my great pleasure in compiling this collection to work with dedicated historians and librarians of historical societies and state and university libraries across the country who so willingly hunted up information, often the same day. There are too many to name here, but their efforts were most appreciated. I must especially thank the librarians of Arlington, Virginia, particularly Dan Cannole, Lynn Kristianson, and Diane Marton and Kristi Beavin of the Children's Room. More thanks go to Celia Blotkamp of the Northern Virginia Speech League; the faculty of Potomac School, especially Cathy Farrell, Christine Hunt, Curt Bland, and Dan Newman; Carol Fonteyn and Joe Lerner; Lydia Schurman; Kirsten Manges and Clyde Taylor; and Kate Bradford and Michelle Whelan, who had many good ideas for the book. And my family, who pitched in when I needed them.

Freedom of speech is indivisible. You cannot deny it to one man and save it for others. Over and over again, the test of our dedication to liberty is our willingness to allow the expression of ideas we hate. If those ideas are lies, the remedy is more speech. . . . The price of liberty to speak the truth as each of us sees it is permitting others the same freedom.

—Archibald Cox

Contents

Introduction

"Is life so dear, or peace so sweet, as to be purchased at the price of chains and slavery? Forbid it, Almighty God! I know not what course others may take; but as for me, give me liberty or give me death."
—Patrick Henry (1775)

Americans in every century have found inspiration in the speech-making of Patrick Henry. His daring address to the Virginia Convention in Richmond, with its famous call to revolution, persuaded the assembled delegates to arm the Virginia militia to resist British oppression, and could have cost him his life had the British won the Revolutionary War.

Some forty years after Patrick Henry's address, Frederick Douglass was born. He was a Maryland slave who would also fight for his freedom, and for the freedom of all slaves in America. He founded an anti-slavery newspaper and entered politics, but his great weapon was his speech-making.

As a boy he owned a book not unlike the one you're now holding, which he bought with the few pennies a slave boy could save. The book was called *The Columbian Orator*, and contained speeches to teach schoolchildren the art of public speaking. The speeches exposed him to exciting ideas about liberty and equality. "Every opportunity I got, I used to read this book," he explained in his autobiography. Although young Frederick was never allowed to go to school, he must have learned from the book, for he became one of the greatest orators the United States ever produced. When he escaped from slavery, the book was one of the few things he took with him.

Oratory such as that of Patrick Henry or Frederick Douglass flourishes wherever you find freedom of speech, a right guaranteed to Americans by the Constitution but withheld from many people of the world who live under dictatorships and totalitarian governments. Events in United States history—slavery, war, women's rights, child labor, the atomic bomb, to mention a few—have always supplied issues to debate. The American town meeting gave people with ideas a place to be heard. And in the days before TV or radio, the speeches of the popular frontier "stump speaker" (who stood on a tree stump to speak) were attended by whole families who traveled miles by wagon to enjoy the scene.

Over a hundred great speeches by Americans are gathered together in this new book of oratory for a new generation of young people. The selection spans almost four centuries of the best of American eloquence, from Powhatan's warning to Captain John Smith in 1609 to Senator Charles Robb's thoughtful reflection, in the year 2000, on the meaning of the flag.

But what is eloquence? Eloquence is the power to persuade with forceful and fluent speech. It relies on passion and straightforwardness for its influence over a crowd. When we read these speeches, we begin to understand why a Chicago newspaper reported that people fought in the halls to get into the courtroom to hear Clarence Darrow speak, and why Martin Luther King wept on hearing President Johnson exclaim "We shall overcome." We can almost see in our mind's eye the thousand tomahawks that early frontiersmen saw brandished by the impassioned hearers of Tecumseh. Sometimes the passion is for a special person, or people, instead of a cause: such as the moving tributes to Lincoln and Lafayette, to the men who fought and died at Gettysburg and Iwo Jima, and to the four innocent girls who died in the bombing of a Birmingham, Alabama, church.

Eloquence always comes from the heart and depends little on a formal education, as true for self-taught Abraham Lincoln as it was for Frederick Douglass. Unschooled American slaves did much for the anti-slavery cause through their speech-making. Native Americans possessed one of the world's richest oratorical traditions despite, or because of, having no written language. Theirs were governments that relied on oral persuasion, with leaders like Big Mouth and Red Jacket who were recognized as great orators not only by their tribes, but also by the Europeans who first encountered them.

You may notice that there are few female speakers before the 1900s in this collection. Women first had to fight for the right to address an audience before they could speak for the reforms (like abolition and women's rights) they hoped to win. For a woman to deliver an address before men remained almost scandalous until 1890. When we read this book from beginning to end we are watching, among other things, the exciting spectacle of women, black Americans, and other minorities breaking free of the laws and traditions that bound them.

One hundred and fifty years after Frederick Douglass, public speaking is still an important skill for leaders of any age. The young people whose speeches appear occasionally in the news—Harry Gladstone and Samantha Smith are two in this book—have found a way to get their passion for reform before the world. We hope these speeches inspire you today, in the same way Frederick Douglass was stirred by the great orators of the past, to speak out yourself for what you believe in.

☆

Powhatan, Chief of the Powhatan Confederacy

To Captain John Smith

Jamestown, Virginia
1609

The first colonists in Jamestown, Virginia, arrived from England in 1607. Building homes and finding food in the New World was difficult, and those who survived the first winters owed their lives to the help they received from the many tribes of the Powhatan Confederacy. However, the settlers took lands for their own use that the Indians considered theirs, and disputes arose over the trading of food and weapons. Chief Wahunsonacock (called Powhatan by the colonists), the father of Pocahontas, warned Captain John Smith against abusing the Indians' friendship.

☆ ☆

I am now grown old, and must soon die; and the succession must descend, in order, to my brothers, Opitchapan, Opekankanough, and Catataugh, and then to my two sisters, and their two daughters. I wish their experience was equal to mine; and that your love to us might not be less than ours to you.

Why should you take by force that from us which you can have by love? Why should you destroy us, who have provided you with food? What can you get by war? We can hide our provisions, and fly into the woods; and then you must consequently famish by wronging your friends. What is the cause of your jealousy? You see us unarmed, and willing to supply your wants, if you will come in a friendly manner, and not with swords and guns, as to invade an enemy.

I am not so simple, as not to know it is better to eat good meat, lie well, and sleep quietly with my women and children; to laugh and be merry with the English; and, being their friend, to have copper, hatchets, and whatever else I want,

5

than to fly from all, to lie cold in the woods, feed upon acorns, roots, and such trash, and to be so hunted, that I cannot rest, eat, or sleep. In such circumstances, my men must watch, and if a twig should but break, all would cry out, "Here comes Captain Smith"; and so, in this miserable manner, to end my miserable life; and, Captain Smith, this might be soon your fate too, through your rashness and unadvisedness.

I, therefore, exhort you to peaceable councils; and, above all, I insist that the guns and swords, the cause of all our jealousy and uneasiness, be removed and sent away.

Big Mouth, Onondaga Chief

To De la Barre, Governor of Canada

New York State, near Lake Ontario
September 1684

Big Mouth is the English translation of Grande Gueule, *the name this Onondaga chief received from the French because he was such an impressive speaker. The Indians pronounced it Garangula. The aged Big Mouth met in what is now New York State with the French governor of Canada, De la Barre (called by the Indians* Yonondio), *who had crossed Lake Ontario with plans to make war on the Five Nations of the Iroquois Confederacy. Big Mouth knew that De la Barre's men were too sick to fight, and he cautioned both De la Barre and New York governor Thomas Dongan (called by the Indians* Corlear) *to preserve the peace. At the end of his address, he presented two beaded wampum belts to make his speech official.*

☆ ☆

Yonondio! I honor you, and the warriors that are with me all likewise honor you. Your interpreter has finished your speech; I now begin mine. My words make haste to reach your ears. Hearken to them. . . .

Hear, Yonondio! What I say is the voice of all the Five Nations. Hear what they answer. Open your ears to what they speak. The Senecas, Cayugas, Onondagas, Oneidas and Mohawks say, that when they buried the hatchet at Cadarackui, in the presence of your predecessor, in the middle of the fort, they planted the tree of peace in the same place, to be there carefully preserved: That in the place of a retreat for soldiers, that fort might be a rendezvous for merchants; that in place of arms and ammunition of war, beavers and merchandize should only enter there.

Hear, Yonondio! Take care for the future that so great a number of soldiers as appear there, do not choke the tree of

7

peace planted in so small a fort. It will be a great loss, if, after it had so easily taken root, you should stop its growth, and prevent its covering your country and ours with its branches. I assure you, in the name of the Five Nations, that our warriors shall dance to the calumet of peace under its leaves. They shall remain quiet on their mats, and shall never dig up the hatchet, till their brother Yonondio, or Corlear, shall either jointly or separately endeavor to attack the country which the Great Spirit has given to our ancestors. This belt preserves my words, and this other the authority which the Five Nations have given me.

Andrew Hamilton

In Defense of John Peter Zenger
and the Freedom of the Press

New York City
August 4, 1735

Andrew Hamilton, born in Scotland, practiced law in Maryland and was later attorney general in Pennsylvania. He defended John Peter Zenger, printer and publisher of the New York Weekly Journal, *when Zenger was arrested for libeling the royal governor of New York, William Cosby. The nearly 70-year-old Hamilton took the case because local lawyers were prevented from defending Zenger. His eloquent defense convinced the jury that the published articles were true and thus not libelous, and Zenger's subsequent acquittal set an important precedent for freedom of the press in the colonies.*

☆ ☆

May it please your honors, I agree with Mr. Attorney [Richard Bradley] that government is a sacred thing, but I differ very widely from him when he would insinuate that the just complaints of men, who suffer under a bad administration, is libeling that administration. . . .

There is heresy in law as well as in religion, and both have changed very much; and we well know that it is not two centuries ago that a man would have burned as a heretic for owning such opinions in matters of religion as are publicly written and printed at this day. . . . I think it is pretty clear that in New York a man may make very free with his God, but he must take special care what he says of his Governor. It is agreed upon by all men that this is a reign of liberty, and while men keep within the bounds of truth, I hope they may with safety both speak and write their sentiments of the conduct of men of power; . . . were this to be denied, then the next step may make them slaves. For what notions can be entertained of slavery beyond that of suffering the greatest injuries and oppressions without the liberty of complaining. . . .

It is said, and insisted upon by Mr. Attorney, that government is a sacred thing, that it is to be supported and reverenced; it is government that protects our persons and estates; that prevents treasons, murders, robberies, riots, and all the train of evils that overturn kingdoms and states and ruin particular persons; and if those in the administration, especially the supreme magistrates, must have all their conduct censured by private men, government cannot subsist. This is called a licentiousness not to be tolerated. It is said that it brings the rulers of the people into contempt so that their authority is not regarded. . . .

But I wish it might be considered at the same time how often it has happened that the abuse of power has been the primary cause of these evils, and that it was the injustice and oppression of these great men which has commonly brought them into contempt with the people. . . .

If a libel is understood in the large and unlimited sense urged by Mr. Attorney, there is scarce a writing I know that may not be called a libel, or scarce any person safe from being called to account as a libeler, for Moses, meek as he was, libeled Cain; and who is it that has not libeled the devil? . . .

The loss of liberty to a generous mind is worse than death; and yet we know there have been those in all ages who, for the sakes of preferment or some imaginary honor, have freely lent a helping hand to oppress, nay, to destroy, their country. . . . Upon the other hand, the man who loves his country prefers its liberty to all other considerations, well knowing that without liberty life is a misery. . . .

Power may justly be compared to a great river; while kept within its bounds, it is both beautiful and useful, but when it overflows its banks, it is then too impetuous to be stemmed; it bears down all before it, and brings destruction and desolation wherever it comes. If, then, this be the nature of power, let us at least do our duty, and, like wise men who value freedom, use our utmost care to support liberty, the only bulwark against lawless power, which, in all ages, has sacrificed to its wild lust and boundless ambition the blood of the best men that ever lived. . . .

I cannot but think it mine and every honest man's duty that, while we pay all due obedience to men in authority, we ought, at the same time, to be upon our guard against power wherever we apprehend that it may affect ourselves or our fellow subjects. . . .

The question before the court, and you, gentlemen of the jury, is not of small nor private concern; it is not the cause of a poor printer, nor of New York alone, which you are now trying. No! It may, in its consequence, affect every free man that lives under a British government on the main continent of America. It is the best cause; it is the cause of liberty. . . .

Every man who prefers freedom to a life of slavery will bless and honor you as men who have baffled the attempt of tyranny, and, by an impartial and uncorrupt verdict, have laid a noble foundation for securing to ourselves, our posterity, and our neighbors that to which nature and the laws of our country have given us a right—the liberty of both exposing and opposing arbitrary power (in these parts of the world at least) by speaking and writing truth.

Canasatego, Onondaga Chief

"We Will Make Men of Them"

Lancaster, Pennsylvania
July 4, 1744

Canasatego was a spokesman for the Six Nations of the Iroquois Confederacy (better known as the Five Nations before the admission of the Tuscarora in about 1722) at the signing of the 1744 Treaty of Lancaster with Pennsylvania, Maryland, and Virginia. His tribe was then offered a chance by the Virginia Legislature to send six of their young men to the College of William and Mary. As he explained to the Virginians, the Native Americans had different ideas from the colonists about what constituted a good education for the young.

We know you highly esteem the kind of Learning taught in these Colleges, and the maintenance of our young Men, while with you, would be very expensive to you. We are convinced, therefore, that you mean to do us Good by your Proposal; and we thank you heartily. But you who are so wise must know that different Nations have different Conceptions of things; and you will not therefore take it amiss, if our Ideas of this kind of Education happens not to be the same with yours.

We have had some experience of it. Several of our young People were formerly brought up in the Colleges of the Northern Provinces; they were instructed in all your Sciences; but, when they came back to us, they were bad Runners, ignorant of every means of living in the Woods, unable to bear either Cold or Hunger, knew neither how to build a Cabin, take a deer, or kill an enemy, spoke our language imperfectly, were therefore neither fit for Hunters, Warriors, nor Counsellors; they were totally good for nothing.

We are however not the less obliged for your kind Offer, tho' we decline accepting it; and to show our grateful Sense of it, if the Gentlemen of Virginia shall send us a Dozen of their Sons, we will take great care of their Education, instruct them in all we know, and make Men of them.

John Hancock

On the Fourth Anniversary of the Boston Massacre

Boston, Massachusetts
March 5, 1774

John Hancock was a leading citizen of Massachusetts who became president of the Continental Congress and was the first signer of the Declaration of Independence. In the years leading up to the Declaration, he spoke forcefully against British treatment of the colonists, and along with Samuel Adams he was wanted under a British warrant of arrest. In this speech, Hancock commemorated the fourth anniversary of the 1770 Boston Massacre, in which King George III's troops had fired on unarmed citizens, killing five Americans.

☆ ☆

It was easy to foresee the consequences which so naturally followed upon [the king] sending troops into America, to enforce obedience to acts of the British Parliament which neither God nor man ever empowered them to make. It was reasonable to expect that troops, who knew the errand they were sent upon, would treat the people whom they were to subjugate with a cruelty and haughtiness which too often buried the honorable character of the soldier in the disgraceful name of an unfeeling ruffian.

The [king's] troops, upon their first arrival, took possession of our senate house, and pointed their cannon against the judgment hall, and even continued them there whilst the supreme court of juridicature for this province was actually sitting to decide upon the lives and fortunes of the king's subjects. Our streets nightly resounded with the noise of riot and debauchery; our peaceful citizens were hourly exposed to shameful insults, and often felt the effects of their violence and outrage. But this was not all; as though they thought it not enough to violate our civil rights, they endeavored to deprive us of the enjoyment of our religious privileges, to vitiate our morals, and thereby render us deserving of destruction. . . .

I come reluctantly to the transactions of that dismal night, when in such quick succession we felt the extremes of grief, astonishment, and rage. . . .

Let this sad tale of death never be told without a tear; let not the heaving bosom cease to burn with a manly indignation at the barbarous story through the long tracts of future time; let every parent tell the shameful story to his listening children until tears of pity glisten in their eyes, and boiling passion shake their tender frames; and whilst the anniversary of that ill-fated night is kept a jubilee in the grim court of pandemonium let all America join in one common prayer to Heaven, that the inhuman, unprovoked murders of the fifth of March, 1770, planned by Hillsborough, and a knot of treacherous knaves in Boston, and executed by the cruel hand of Preston and his sanguinary coadjutors, may ever stand in history without parallel.

But what, my countrymen, withheld the ready arm of vengeance from executing instant justice on the vile assassins? . . . May that generous compassion which often preserves from ruin even a guilty villain, forever actuate the noble bosoms of Americans. But let not the miscreant host vainly imagine that we feared their arms. No, them we despised; we dread nothing but slavery. Death is the creature of a poltroon's brain; 'tis immortality to sacrifice ourselves for the salvation of our country.

We fear not death. That gloomy night, the pale-faced moon, and the affrighted stars that hurried through the sky, can witness that we fear not death. Our hearts which, at the recollection, glow with rage that four revolving years have scarcely taught us to restrain, can witness that we fear not death; and happy it is for those who dared to insult us, that their naked bones are not now piled up an everlasting monument of Massachusetts' bravery.

☆

Logan, Mingo Chief

To Lord Dunmore

Near Chillicothe, Ohio
October 1774

Logan was long loyal to the colonists, taking no part in the French and Indian Wars. But in May of 1774, when members of his family and tribe were killed by whites near Wheeling, West Virginia, Logan's tribe retaliated against local settlers. Lord Dunmore, governor of Virginia, then marched with troops to fight the Indians in a campaign known as Dunmore's War. After the battle of Point Pleasant, Logan refused to participate in peace negotiations, sending an address to be delivered by Dunmore's messengers. The speech became famous for its simple eloquence—though Logan would later discover that it was not Michael Cresap who murdered his family.

☆ ☆

I appeal to any white man to say if he ever entered Logan's cabin hungry and he gave him not meat; if he ever came cold and naked and he clothed him not.

During the course of the last long and bloody war, Logan remained idle in his cabin, an advocate for peace. Such was my love for the whites that my countrymen pointed as I passed and said, "Logan is a friend of the white man." I had even thought to have lived with you but for the injuries of one man.

Colonel Cresap, the last spring in cold blood and unprovoked, murdered the relatives of Logan, not even sparing his wives and children. There runs not a drop of my blood in the veins of any living creature.

This called on me for revenge. I have sought it. I have killed many. I have fully glutted my vengeance. For my country I rejoice in the beams of peace; but do not harbor a thought that mine is the joy of fear. Logan never felt fear. He will not turn on his heel to save his life. Who is there to mourn for Logan? Not one.

Patrick Henry

"Give Me Liberty or Give Me Death"

Richmond, Virginia
March 23, 1775

Patrick Henry was a self-taught lawyer who served for many years in the Virginia House of Burgesses and became famous for his superb oratory. At the second Virginia Convention of Delegates assembled in Richmond's St. John's Church, Henry introduced a radical resolution urging that Virginia prepare to arm and defend itself against British oppression. His speech electrified his audience, and as he spoke the splendid last lines, he thrust an imaginary dagger into his chest and fell back into his seat. No written record of the speech existed until it was reconstructed forty years later by William Wirt, Henry's biographer.

Mr. President: No man thinks more highly than I do of the patriotism, as well as abilities of the very worthy gentlemen who have just addressed the House. But different men often see the same subject in different lights; and, therefore, I hope that it will not be thought disrespectful to those gentlemen, if, entertaining as I do, opinions of a character very opposite to theirs, I shall speak forth my sentiments freely and without reserve. This is no time for ceremony. The question before the House is one of awful moment to this country. For my own part I consider it as nothing less than a question of freedom or slavery. . . .

Mr. President, it is natural to man to indulge in the illusions of hope. We are apt to shut our eyes against a painful truth. . . . For my part, whatever anguish of spirit it may cost, I am willing to know the whole truth; to know the worst and to provide for it.

I have but one lamp by which my feet are guided; and that is the lamp of experience. I know of no way of judging of the future but by the past. And judging by the past, I wish to know what there has been in the conduct of the British ministry for the last ten years, to justify those hopes with which gentlemen have been pleased to solace themselves and the House? Is it that insidious smile with which our petition has been lately received? Trust it not, sir; it will prove a snare to your feet. Suffer not yourselves to be betrayed with a kiss. Ask yourselves how this gracious reception of our petition comports with these war-like preparations which cover our waters and darken our land. Are fleets and armies necessary to a work of love and reconciliation? Have we shown ourselves so unwilling to be reconciled, that force must be called in to win back our love? Let us not deceive ourselves, sir. These are the implements of war and subjugation; the last arguments to which kings resort.

I ask gentlemen, sir, what means this martial array, if its purpose be not to force us to submission? Can gentlemen assign any other possible motives for it? Has Great Britain any enemy, in this quarter of the world, to call for all this accumulation of navies and armies? No, sir, she has none. They are meant for us; they can be meant for no other. They are sent over to bind and rivet upon us those chains which the British ministry have been so long forging. . . . Let us not, I beseech you, sir, deceive ourselves longer.

Sir, we have done everything that could be done, to avert the storm which is now coming on. We have petitioned; we have remonstrated; we have supplicated; we have prostrated ourselves before the throne, and have implored its interposition to arrest the tyrannical hands of the ministry and Parliament. Our petitions have been slighted; our remonstrances have produced additional violence and insult; our supplications have been disregarded; and we have been spurned, with contempt, from the foot of the throne. In vain, after these things, may we indulge the fond hope of peace and reconciliation. There is no longer any room for hope. If we wish to be free, . . . we must fight! I repeat it, sir, we must fight! An appeal to arms and to the God of Hosts is all that is left us!

They tell us, sir, that we are weak; unable to cope with so formidable an adversary. But when shall we be stronger? Will it be the next week, or the next year? Will it be when we are totally disarmed, and when a British guard shall be stationed in every house? Shall we gather strength by irresolution and inaction? Shall we acquire the means of effectual resistance, by lying supinely on our backs, and hugging the delusive phantom of hope, until our enemies shall have bound us hand and foot?

Sir, we are not weak, if we make proper use of the means which the God of nature hath placed in our power. Three millions of people, armed in the holy cause of liberty, and in such a country as that which we possess, are invincible by any force which our enemy can send against us. Besides, sir, we shall not fight our battles alone. There is a just God who presides over the destinies of nations; and who will raise up friends to fight our battles for us. The battle, sir, is not to the strong alone; it is to the vigilant, the active, the brave.

Besides, sir, we have no election. If we were base enough to desire it, it is now too late to retire from the contest. There is no retreat, but in submission and slavery! Our chains are forged! Their clanking may be heard on the plains of Boston! The war is inevitable—and let it come! I repeat it, sir, let it come!

It is in vain, sir, to extenuate the matter. Gentlemen may cry peace, peace—but there is no peace. The war is actually begun! The next gale that sweeps from the north will bring to our ears the clash of resounding arms! Our brethren are already in the field! Why stand we here idle? What is it that gentlemen wish? What would they have? Is life so dear, or peace so sweet, as to be purchased at the price of chains and slavery? Forbid it, Almighty God! I know not what course others may take; but as for me, give me liberty, or give me death!

☆

Solomon, Stockbridge Chief

"We Have Ever Been True Friends"

Stockbridge, Massachusetts
April 11, 1775

Though the French and the British had both earlier made allies of the Indians, the Continental Congress hesitated to do so. Massachusetts was the first state to accept their services at the onset of the Revolutionary War, when sixty Stockbridge warriors enrolled in Minuteman regiments. Solomon, a chief of the Stockbridge, addressed the delegate of the Massachusetts Provincial Congress, offering help against the British.

☆ ☆

Brothers! You remember, when you first came over the great waters, I was great and you were little; very small. I then took you in for a friend, and kept you under my arms, so that no one might injure you. Since that time we have ever been true friends; there has never been any quarrel between us. But now our conditions are changed. You are become great and tall. You reach to the clouds. You are seen all round the world. I am become small; very little. I am not so high as your knee. Now you take care of me; and I look to you for protection.

Brothers! I am sorry to hear of this great quarrel between you and Old England. It appears that blood must soon be shed to end this quarrel. We never till this day understood the foundation of this quarrel between you and the country you came from.

Brothers! Whenever I see your blood running, you will soon find me about you to revenge my brother's blood. Although I am low and very small, I will grip hold of your enemy's heel, that he cannot run so fast, and so light, as if he had nothing at his heels. . . .

Brothers! One thing I ask of you, if you send for me to fight, that you will let me fight in my own Indian way. I am not used to fight English fashion; therefore you must not expect I can train like your men. Only point out to me where your enemies keep, and that is all I shall want to know.

Samuel Adams

To the Continental Congress

Philadelphia, Pennsylvania
August 1, 1776

Samuel Adams was a member of the Massachusetts legislature, the organizer of the Boston Tea Party, and the firebrand behind the American Revolution. He served as a delegate from Massachusetts to the second Continental Congress in Philadelphia, an assembly of representatives from each colony who met to air grievances against the British and to form the Continental Army. A month after they adopted the Declaration of Independence, on July 4, 1776, and the day before they fixed their signatures to the historic document, Adams rose in the assembly to assure the delegates of his confidence in their ability to win the war against Britain.

☆ ☆

We are now on this continent, to the astonishment of the world, three millions of souls united in one cause. We have large armies, well disciplined and appointed, with commanders inferior to none in military skill, and superior in activity and zeal. We are furnished with arsenals and stores beyond our most sanguine expectations, and foreign nations are waiting to crown our success by their alliances. There are instances of, I would say, an almost astonishing Providence in our favor; our success has staggered our enemies, and almost given faith to infidels; so we may truly say it is not our own arm which has saved us.

The hand of Heaven appears to have led us on to be, perhaps, humble instruments and means in the great providential dispensation which is completing. We have fled from the political Sodom; let us not look back, lest we perish and become a monument of infamy and derision to the world. For can we ever expect more unanimity and a better preparation for defense; more infatuation of counsel among our enemies, and more valor and zeal among ourselves? The same force and resistance which are sufficient to procure us our liberties will secure us a glorious independence and support us in the dignity of free, imperial states.

We cannot suppose that our opposition has made a corrupt and dissipated nation more friendly to America, or created in them a greater respect for the rights of mankind. We can therefore expect a restoration and establishment of our privileges, and a compensation for the injuries we have received, from their want of power, from their fears, and not from their virtues. The unanimity and valor which will effect an honorable peace can render a future contest for our liberties unnecessary. He who has strength to chain down the wolf is a madman if he let him loose without drawing his teeth and paring his nails.

We have no other alternative than independence, or the most ignominious and galling servitude. The legions of our enemies thicken on our plains; desolation and death mark their bloody career; whilst the mangled corpses of our countrymen seem to cry out to us as a voice from Heaven.

Our union is now complete; our constitution composed, established, and approved. You are now the guardians of your own liberties. We may justly address you, as the *decemviri* did the Romans, and say: "Nothing that we propose can pass into a law without your consent. Be yourselves, O Americans, the authors of those laws on which your happiness depends."

You have now in the field armies sufficient to repel the whole force of your enemies and their base and mercenary auxiliaries. The hearts of your soldiers beat high with the spirit of freedom; they are animated with the justice of their cause, and while they grasp their swords can look up to Heaven for assistance. Your adversaries are composed of wretches who laugh at the rights of humanity, who turn religion into derision, and would, for higher wages, direct their swords against their leaders or their country.

Go on, then, in your generous enterprise, with gratitude to Heaven for past success, and confidence of it in the future. For my own part, I ask no greater blessing than to share with you the common danger and common glory. If I have a wish dearer to my soul than that my ashes may be mingled with those of a Warren and a Montgomery, it is that these American States may never cease to be free and independent.

Benjamin Franklin

To the Constitutional Convention

Philadelphia, Pennsylvania
September 17, 1787

Benjamin Franklin—scientist, printer, postmaster, diplomat, commonsense philosopher—proved to be one of the great statesmen of the Revolutionary War. He helped draft the Declaration of Independence and was one of its signers, and was sent in 1787 as a Pennsylvania delegate to the Constitutional Convention. The writing of the Constitution took months of debate and compromise, and Franklin urged the Convention members to sign it, arguing that though it might have faults there was not likely to be another better. The frail elder statesman, then in his eighties, asked James Wilson, another delegate from Pennsylvania, to read his address for him. The Constitution was approved soon after.

☆ ☆

Mr. President, I confess that I do not entirely approve of this Constitution at present, but, sir, I am not sure I shall never approve it: for, having lived long, I have experienced many instances of being obliged, by better information or fuller consideration, to change opinions even on important subjects, which I once thought right, but found to be otherwise. It is therefore that the older I grow, the more apt I am to doubt my own judgment, and to pay more respect to the judgment of others.

Most men, indeed, as well as most sects in religion, think themselves in possession of all truth, and that wherever others differ from them it is so far error. Steele, a Protestant, in a dedication tells the pope that the only difference between our two churches, in their opinions of the certainty of their doctrine, is, the Romish church is infallible and the Church of England is never in the wrong. But though many private persons think almost as highly of their own infallibility as of that of their sect, few express it so naturally as a certain French lady, who in a little dispute with her sister, said, I don't know how it happens, Sister, but I meet with nobody but myself that's *always* in the right.

In these sentiments, sir I agree to this Constitution, with all its faults, if they are such; because I think a general government necessary for us. . . . I doubt, too, whether any other convention we can obtain may be able to make a better constitution: for when you assemble a number of men to have the advantage of their joint wisdom, you inevitably assemble with those men all their prejudices, their passions, their errors of opinion, their local interests, and their selfish views. From such an assembly can a perfect production be expected? It therefore astonishes me, sir, to find this system approaching so near to perfection as it does; and I think it will astonish our enemies, who are waiting with confidence to hear that our councils are confounded, like those of the builders of Babel, and that our states are on the point of separation, only to meet hereafter for the purpose of cutting one another's throats.

Thus I consent, sir, to this Constitution because I expect no better, and because I am not sure that it is not the best. The opinions I have had of its errors, I sacrifice to the public good. I have never whispered a syllable of them abroad. Within these walls they were born, and here they shall die. If every one of us in returning to our constituents were to report the objections he has had to it, and use his influence to gain partisans in support of them, we might prevent its being generally received. . . .

Much of the strength and efficiency of any government, in procuring and securing happiness to the people depends on opinion, on the general opinion of the goodness of that government as well as of the wisdom and integrity of its governors. I hope therefore that for our own sakes, as a part of the people, and for the sake of our posterity, we shall act heartily and unanimously in recommending this constitution, wherever our influence may extend, and turn our future thoughts and endeavors to the means of having it well administered.

On the whole, sir, I cannot help expressing a wish that every member of the convention who may still have objections to it would with me on this occasion doubt a little of his own infallibility, and, to make *manifest* our *unanimity*, put his name to this instrument.

☆

Jonathan Smith

To the Massachusetts Convention

Boston, Massachusetts
January 25, 1788

After the new federal Constitution was approved by the Constitutional Convention in 1787, each state had to ratify the document. When the Massachusetts convention met for this purpose, many anti-federalist delegates expressed concerns about a strong federal government. Jonathan Smith, delegate from Lanesboro, Berkshire County, was an unschooled farmer who saw merit in the document, and he told the delegates so in plain language. The "black cloud" he refers to was Shays's Rebellion, a farmers' revolt the previous year, that had happened partly because of the state's failure to ease taxes in the economic depression following the Revolution.

☆ ☆

Mr. President. I am a plain man, and get my living by the plough. I am not used to speak in public, but I beg your leave to say a few words to my brother ploughjoggers in this house. I have lived in a part of the country where I have known the worth of good government by the want of it. There was a black cloud that rose in the east last winter and spread out over the west.

I mean, sir, the county of Bristol; the cloud rose there, and burst upon us, and produced a dreadful effect. It brought on a state of anarchy, and that led to tyranny. I say it brought anarchy. People that used to live peaceably and were before good neighbors, got distracted and took up arms against government. . . .

Had any person, that was able to protect us, come and set up his standard, we should have flocked to it, even if it had been a monarch; and that monarch might have proved a tyrant; so that you see that anarchy leads to tyranny, and better have one tyrant than so many at once.

Now, Mr. President, when I saw this Constitution, I found that it was a cure for these disorders. It was just such a thing as we wanted. I got a copy of it, and read it over and over. I had been a member of the Convention to form our own state Constitution, and had learnt something about the checks and balances of power, and I found them all here. I did not go to any lawyer, to ask his opinion; we have no lawyer in our town, and we do well enough without. I formed my own opinion, and was pleased with this Constitution. My honorable old daddy there [Amos Singletary], won't think that I expect to be a Congressman, and swallow up the liberties of the people. I never had any post, nor do I want one. But I don't think the worse of the Constitution because lawyers, and men of learning, and moneyed men, are fond of it. I don't suspect that they want to get into Congress and abuse their power. I am not of such a jealous make. They that are honest men themselves are not apt to suspect other people. I don't know why our constituents have not as good a right to be jealous of us as we seem to be of the Congress; and I think those gentlemen, who are so very suspicious that as soon as a man gets into power he turns rogue, had better look at home.

We are, by this Constitution, allowed to send ten members to Congress. Have we not more than that number fit to go? I dare say, if we pick out ten, we shall have another ten left, and I hope ten times ten; and will not these be a check upon those that go? Will they go to Congress and abuse their power, and do mischief, when they know they must return and look the other ten in the face, and be called to account for their conduct? Some gentlemen think that our liberty and property are not safe in the hands of moneyed men, and men of learning. I am not of that mind.

Brother farmers, let us suppose a case: Suppose you had a farm of 50 acres, and your title was disputed, and there was a farm of 5000 acres joined to you, that belonged to a man of learning, and his title was involved in the same difficulty; would you not be glad to have him for your friend, rather than stand alone in the dispute? Well, the case is the same. These lawyers, these moneyed men, these men of learning, are all embarked in the same cause with us, and we must all swim or sink together. And shall we throw the Constitution overboard because it does not please us alike? Suppose two or three of you had been at pains to break up a piece of rough land, and sow it with wheat; would you let it lie waste because you could not agree what sort of a fence to make? Would it not be better to put up a fence that did not please every one's fancy, rather than not fence it at all, or keep disputing about it until the wild beasts came in and devoured it?

Some gentlemen say, "Don't be in a hurry; take time to consider"; and "Don't take a leap in the dark." I say, "Take things in time; gather fruit when it is ripe." There is a time to sow and a time to reap; we sowed our seed when we sent men to the Federal Convention; now is the harvest. Now is the time to reap the fruit of our labor. And if we won't do it now, I am afraid we never shall have another opportunity.

George Washington

"Observe Good Faith and Justice towards All Nations"

Philadelphia, Pennsylvania
September 19, 1796

After presiding over the Constitutional Convention, George Washington served two terms as the first president, from 1789 to 1797. The enormously popular Revolutionary War general and president was later called the "Father of His Country," and eulogized by Henry Lee as "First in war, first in peace, and first in the hearts of his countrymen." Before retiring to his home at Mt. Vernon, Washington delivered to Congress a Farewell Address in which he offered advice on the path the young country should follow in its interaction with foreign governments.

☆ ☆

Observe good faith and justice towards all nations. Cultivate peace and harmony with all. Religion and morality enjoin this conduct, and can it be that good policy does not equally enjoin it? It will be worthy of a free, enlightened, and, at no distant period, a great nation to give to mankind the magnanimous and too novel example of a people always guided by an exalted justice and benevolence. Who can doubt that in the course of time and things the fruits of such a plan would richly repay any temporary advantages which might be lost by a steady adherence to it? . . .

In the execution of such a plan nothing is more essential than that permanent, inveterate antipathies against particular nations and passionate attachments for others should be excluded, and that in place of them just and amicable feelings towards all should be cultivated. The nation which indulges towards another an habitual hatred, or an habitual fondness, is in some degree a slave. It is a slave to its animosity or to its affection, either of which is sufficient to lead it astray from its duty and its interest. . . .

So likewise, a passionate attachment of one nation for another produces a variety of evils. Sympathy for the favorite nation, facilitating the illusion of an imaginary common interest, in cases where no real common interest exists, and infusing into one the enmities of the other, betrays the former into a participation in the quarrels and wars of the latter, without adequate inducement or justification. It leads also to concessions to the favorite nation of privileges denied to others, which is apt doubly to injure the nation making the concessions; by unnecessarily parting with what ought to have been retained; and by exciting jealousy, ill will, and a disposition to retaliate, in the parties from whom equal privileges are withheld. . . .

Against the insidious wiles of foreign influence (I conjure you to believe me, fellow citizens), the jealousy of a free people ought to be *constantly* awake, since history and experience prove that foreign influence is one of the most baneful foes of republican government. But that jealousy to be useful must be impartial; else it becomes the instrument of the very influence to be avoided, instead of a defense against it. . . .

'Tis our true policy to steer clear of permanent alliances, with any portion of the foreign world. . . . Taking care always to keep ourselves, by suitable establishments, in a respectable defensive posture, we may safely trust to temporary alliances for extraordinary emergencies.

Harmony, and a liberal intercourse with all nations, are recommended by policy, humanity, and interest. But even our commercial policy should hold an equal and impartial hand: neither seeking nor granting exclusive favors or preferences; . . . constantly keeping in view, that 'tis folly in one nation to look for disinterested favors from another; that it must pay with a portion of its independence for whatever it may accept under that character; that by such acceptance, it may place itself in the condition of having given equivalents for nominal favors and yet of being reproached with ingratitude for not giving more. There can be no greater error than to expect, or calculate upon, real favors from nation to nation. 'Tis an illusion which experience must cure, which a just pride ought to discard.

In offering to you, my countrymen, these counsels of an old and affectionate friend, I dare not hope they will make the strong and lasting impression I could wish, that they will control the usual current of the passions, or prevent our nation from running the course which has hitherto marked the destiny of nations. But if I may even flatter myself that they may be productive of some partial benefit, some occasional good; that they may now and then recur to moderate the fury of party spirit, to warn against the mischiefs of foreign intrigue, to guard against the impostures of pretended patriotism; this hope will be a full recompense for the solicitude for your welfare, by which they have been dictated.

☆

Thomas Jefferson

First Inaugural Address

Washington, D.C.
March 4, 1801

Thomas Jefferson—statesman, philosopher, scientist, inventor, architect, diplomat, and author of the Declaration of Independence—became the third president of the United States in 1801. In the presidential race, Jefferson's Republicans had beaten the Federalists handily, but Jefferson himself was tied with Aaron Burr in a deadlock that was finally broken in the House of Representatives. His inaugural address sought to heal the political divisions between the two parties, and set out his view of the primary concerns of government. Jefferson's was the first inauguration held in the new capital city of Washington.

☆ ☆

About to enter, fellow citizens, upon the exercise of duties which comprehend everything dear and valuable to you, it is proper you should understand what I deem the essential principles of our government and, consequently, those which ought to shape its administration. I will compress them within the narrowest compass they will bear, stating the general principle, but not all its limitations.

Equal and exact justice to all men, of whatever state or persuasion, religious or political; peace, commerce, and honest friendship with all nations, entangling alliances with none; the support of the state governments in all their rights, as the most competent administrations for our domestic concerns, and the surest bulwarks against antirepublican tendencies; the preservation of the general government in its whole constitutional vigor, as the sheet anchor of our peace at home and safety abroad; a jealous care of the right of election by the people, a mild and safe corrective of abuses which are lopped by the sword of revolution where peaceable remedies are unprovided; absolute acquiescence in the decisions of the majority, the vital principle of republics, from which there is no appeal but to force, the vital principle and immediate parent of despotism; a well-disciplined militia, our best reliance in peace, and for the first moments of war, till regulars may relieve them; the supremacy of the civil over the military authority; economy in the public expense, that labor may be lightly burdened; the honest payment of our debts and sacred preservation of the public faith; encouragement of agriculture, and of commerce as its handmaid; the diffusion of information, and arraignment of all abuses at the bar of the public reason; freedom of religion; freedom of the press, and freedom of person, under the protection of the habeas corpus, and trial by juries impartially selected.

These principles form the bright constellation which has gone before us, and guided our steps through an age of revolution and reformation. The wisdom of our sages, and blood of our heroes, have been devoted to their attainment. They should be the creed of our political faith, the text of civic instruction, the touchstone by which to try the services of those we trust; and should we wander from them in moments of error or of alarm, let us hasten to retrace our steps and to regain the road which alone leads to peace, liberty, and safety.

Red Jacket, Seneca Chief

"We Never Quarrel about Religion"

Buffalo, New York
Summer 1805

Red Jacket of the Senecas was one of the greatest Native American orators, as proud of his speaking ability as he was of being a warrior. He liked to wear a red coat he received from the British during the Revolutionary War, but he otherwise shunned the customs of whites and promoted the traditional way of life for his people. At a conference of chiefs of the Senecas at Buffalo Creek, he used clear logic and diplomacy to rebuff the efforts of Reverend Cram, a Boston missionary of the Moravian Church, to convert his tribe to Christianity.

☆ ☆

Brother!—This council fire was kindled by you. It was at your request that we came together at this time. We have listened with attention to what you have said. You requested us to speak our minds freely. This gives us great joy, for we now consider that we stand upright before you, and can speak what we think. All have heard your voice, and all speak to you as one man. Our minds are agreed. . . .

Brother!—Listen to what we say. There was a time when our forefathers owned this great island. Their seats extended from the rising to the setting sun. The Great Spirit had made it for the use of Indians. He had created the buffalo, the deer, and other animals for food. He made the bear and the beaver, and their skins served us for clothing. He had scattered them over the country, and taught us how to take them. He had caused the earth to produce corn for bread. All this he had done for his red children because he loved them. If we had any disputes about hunting-grounds, they were generally settled without the shedding of much blood. But an evil day came upon us. Your forefathers crossed the great waters, and landed on this island. Their numbers were small. They found friends and not enemies. They told us they had fled from their own country for fear of wicked men, and come here to enjoy their religion. They asked for a small seat. We took pity on them, granted their request, and they sat down amongst us. We gave them corn and meat. They gave us poison in return. . . .

At length their numbers had greatly increased. They wanted more land. They wanted our country. Our eyes were opened, and our minds became uneasy. Wars took place. Indians were hired to fight against Indians, and many of our people were destroyed. They also brought strong liquors among us. It was strong and powerful, and has slain thousands.

Brother!—Our seats were once large, and yours were very small. You have now become a great people, and we have scarcely a place left to spread our blankets. You have got our country, but are not satisfied. You want to force your religion upon us.

Brother!—Continue to listen. You say that you are sent to instruct us how to worship the Great Spirit agreeably to his mind; and if we do not take hold of the religion which you white people teach, we shall be unhappy hereafter. You say that you are right and we are lost. How do we know this to be true? We understand that your religion is written in a book. If it was intended for us as well as for you, why has not the Great Spirit given it to us; and not only to us, but why did he not give to our forefathers the knowledge of that book, with the means of understanding it rightly? We only know what you tell us about it. How shall we know when to believe, being so often deceived by the white people.

Brother!—You say there is but one way to worship and serve the Great Spirit. If there is but one religion, why do you white people differ so much about it? Why not all agree, as you can all read the book?

Brother!—We do not understand these things. We are told that your religion was given to your forefathers, and has been handed down from father to son. We also have a religion which was given to our forefathers, and has been handed down to us their children. We worship that way. It teaches us to be thankful for all the favors we receive, to love each other, and to be united. We never quarrel about religion. . . .

Brother!—We do not wish to destroy your religion, or take it from you. We only want to enjoy our own.

Tecumseh, Shawnee Chief

"Sleep Not Longer, O Choctaws and Chickasaws"

Mississippi
September 1811

The great Shawnee Chief Tecumseh had the deep respect of the U.S. officials who heard his magnificent speeches and observed his tireless efforts on behalf of native peoples. He traveled extensively with a body of warriors among tribes from Iowa to Florida, campaigning to gather support for a confederation to halt land sales to the U.S. government. On a tour through the South he addressed the Choctaws and Chickasaws of Mississippi, urging them to join him on the side of the British, but the Choctaw Chief Pushmataha successfully reminded his warriors that their future lay with the Americans. Tecumseh fought on the side of the British in the War of 1812 and died in battle.

☆ ☆

In view of questions of vast importance, have we met together in solemn council tonight. Nor should we here debate whether we have been wronged and injured, but by what measures we should avenge ourselves. . . .

The whites are already nearly a match for us all united, and too strong for any one tribe alone to resist; so that unless we support one another with our collective and united forces; unless every tribe unanimously combines to give check to the ambition and avarice of the whites, they will soon conquer us apart and disunited, and we will be driven away from our native country and scattered as autumnal leaves before the wind.

But have we not courage enough remaining to defend our country and maintain our ancient independence? Will we calmly suffer the white intruders and tyrants to enslave us? Shall it be said of our race that we knew not how to extricate ourselves from the three most dreadful calamities—folly, inactivity and cowardice?

But what need is there to speak of the past? It speaks for itself and asks, Where today is the Pequod? Where the Narragansetts, the Mohawks, Pocanokets, and many other once powerful tribes of our race? They have vanished before the avarice and oppression of the white men, as snow before a summer sun. In the vain hope of alone defending their ancient possessions, they have fallen in the wars with the white men. Look abroad over their once beautiful country, and what see you now? Naught but the ravages of the pale face destroyers meet our eyes.

So it will be with you Choctaws and Chickasaws! Soon your mighty forest trees, under the shade of whose wide spreading branches you have played in infancy, sported in boyhood, and now rest your wearied limbs after the fatigue of the chase, will be cut down to fence in the land which the white intruders dare to call their own. Soon their broad roads will pass over the grave of your fathers, and the place of their rest will be blotted out forever.

The annihilation of our race is at hand unless we unite in one common cause against the common foe. Think not, brave Choctaws and Chickasaws, that you can remain passive and indifferent to the common danger, and thus escape the common fate. Your people, too, will soon be as falling leaves and scattering clouds before their blighting breath. You, too, will be driven away from your native land and ancient domains as leaves are driven before the wintry storms.

Sleep not longer, O Choctaws and Chickasaws, in false security and delusive hopes. Our broad domains are fast escaping from our grasp. Every year our white intruders become more greedy, exacting, oppressive and overbearing. Every year contentions spring up between them and our people and when blood is shed we have to make atonement whether right or wrong, at the cost of the lives of our greatest chiefs, and the yielding up of large tracts of our lands.

Before the palefaces came among us, we enjoyed the happiness of unbounded freedom, and were acquainted with

neither riches, wants nor oppression. How is it now? Wants
and oppression are our lot; for are we not controlled in everything, and dare we move without asking, by your leave? Are
we not being stripped day by day of the little that remains of
our ancient liberty? Do they not even kick and strike us as
they do their black-faces? How long will it be before they will
tie us to a post and whip us, and make us work for them in
their corn fields as they do them? Shall we wait for that
moment or shall we die fighting before submitting to such
ignominy? . . .

Will we not soon be driven from our respective countries
and the graves of our ancestors? Will not the bones of our
dead be plowed up, and their graves be turned into fields?
Shall we calmly wait until they become so numerous that we
will no longer be able to resist oppression? Will we wait to be
destroyed in our turn, without making an effort worthy of our
race? Shall we give up our homes, our country, bequeathed to
us by the Great Spirit, the graves of our dead, and everything
that is dear and sacred to us, without a struggle?

I know you will cry with me: Never! Never! Then let us by
unity of action destroy them all, which we now can do, or
drive them back whence they came. . . . Let us form one body,
one heart, and defend to the last warrior our country, our
homes, our liberty, and the graves of our fathers.

☆

Pushmataha, Choctaw Chief

Welcome to Lafayette

Washington, D.C.
December 12, 1824

Pushmataha was the venerated chief of the peaceable Choctaws of Mississippi who defied Tecumseh's call to make war on the Americans during the War of 1812. With General Andrew Jackson, he fought the British in the victorious Battle of New Orleans in 1815, and he became known as "the Indian General." He was sixty when he delivered this tribute to Lafayette as part of a delegation welcoming the sixty-seven-year-old Revolutionary War general on his last visit to America from France. Pushmataha died shortly afterward in Washington and received a full military burial in Congressional Cemetery. The address was chosen by the orator William Jennings Bryan for his own book of the world's great speeches.

☆ ☆

Nearly fifty snows have melted since you drew sword as a champion of Washington. With him you fought the enemy of America, and proved yourself a warrior. After you finished the war you returned to your own country, and now you are come back to visit the land where you are honored by a numerous and powerful people.

You see everywhere the children of those by whose side you went to battle, crowding around you and shaking your hand, as the hand of a father. We have had these things told us in our villages, and our hearts have longed to see you.

We have come; we have taken you by the hand and are satisfied. This is the first time we have seen you; it will probably be the last. We have no more to say. The earth will part us forever.

Daniel Webster

Bunker Hill Oration

Charlestown, Massachusetts
June 17, 1825

As a young man Daniel Webster devoted himself to the study of speech-making. He never achieved his ambition of being elected president, but he was widely considered the greatest orator of his day. He served as senator from Massachusetts and later as secretary of state, and he labored always to keep the northern and southern states in the Union. As a U.S. congressman, and with Lafayette in attendance, he gave the address at the laying of the cornerstone for the Bunker Hill Monument, which memorialized the fiftieth anniversary of the brave but losing engagement of American forces against the British in the Revolutionary War Battle of Bunker Hill.

☆ ☆

We are among the sepulchers of our fathers. We are on ground distinguished by their valor, their constancy, and the shedding of their blood. . . .

The great event, in the history of the continent, which we are now met here to commemorate—that prodigy of modern times, at once the wonder and the blessing of the world—is the American Revolution. In a day of extraordinary prosperity and happiness, of high national honor, distinction, and power, we are brought together, in this place, by our love of country, by our admiration of exalted character, by our gratitude for signal services and patriotic devotion. . . .

When Louis XIV said, "I am the state," he expressed the essence of the doctrine of unlimited power. By the rules of that system, the people are disconnected from the state; they are its subjects; it is their lord. These ideas, founded in the love of power, and long supported by the excess and the abuse of it, are yielding in our age to other opinions; and the civilized world seems at last to be proceeding to the conviction of that fundamental and manifest truth, that the powers of government are but a trust, and that they cannot be lawfully exercised but for the good of the community. . . .

We may hope that the growing influence of enlightened sentiments will promote the permanent peace of the world. Wars, . . . if not less likely to happen at all, will be less likely to become general and involve many nations, as the great principle shall be more and more established, that the interest of the world is peace, and its first great statute, that every nation possesses the power of establishing a government for itself. . . . Thus far our example shows that such governments are compatible, not only with respectability and power, but with repose, with peace, with security of personal rights, with good laws and a just administration.

We are not propagandists. Wherever other systems are preferred, either as being thought better in themselves or as better suited to existing conditions, we leave the preference to be enjoyed. Our history hitherto proves, however, that the popular form is practicable and that, with wisdom and knowledge, men may govern themselves; and the duty incumbent on us is to preserve the consistency of this cheering example and take care that nothing may weaken its authority with the world. If in our case the representative system ultimately fail, popular governments must be pronounced impossible. No combination of circumstances more favorable to the experiment can ever be expected to occur. The last hopes of mankind, therefore, rest with us; and if it should be proclaimed that our example had become an argument against the experiment, the knell of popular liberty would be sounded throughout the earth. . . .

Let the sacred obligations which have devolved on this generation and on us sink deep into our hearts. Those are daily dropping from among us who established our liberty and our government. The great trust now descends to new hands. . . . Let our age be the age of improvement. In a day of peace let us advance the arts of peace and the works of peace. Let us develop the resources of our land, call forth its powers, build up its institutions, promote all its great interests, and see whether we also, in our day and generation, may not perform something worthy to be remembered. Let us cultivate a true spirit of union and harmony. In pursuing the great objects which our condition points out to us, let us act under a settled conviction, and a habitual feeling that these twenty-four states are one country. . . .

Let our object be our country, our whole country, and nothing but our country. And by the blessing of God may that country itself become a vast and splendid monument, not of oppression and terror, but of wisdom, of peace, and of liberty, upon which the world may gaze with admiration, forever.

Black Hawk, Sauk Chief

"Farewell to Black Hawk"

Prairie du Chien, Wisconsin
August 3, 1832

Black Hawk of the Sauk (or Sac) allied himself with the British against the Americans in the War of 1812. Later he declared unjust a treaty he had signed with the Americans that required his tribe to move off their lands in Illinois. The Indian Removal Act of 1830 nevertheless forced the Indians to move west across the Mississippi River. Hostilities with the U.S. Army, known as the Black Hawk War, began when Black Hawk was found returning with his followers. He was captured in Wisconsin after the slaughter of much of his tribe, and he made this address on his surrender to General Henry Atkinson.

You have taken me prisoner with all my warriors. I am much grieved, for I expected, if I did not defeat you, to hold out much longer, and give you more trouble before I surrendered. . . .

I fought hard. But your guns were well aimed. The bullets flew like birds in the air, and whizzed by our ears like the wind through the trees in the winter. My warriors fell around me; it began to look dismal. I saw my evil day at hand. The sun rose dim on us in the morning, and at night it sunk in a dark cloud, and looked like a ball of fire. That was the last sun that shone on Black Hawk. His heart is dead, and no longer beats quick in his bosom. He is now a prisoner to the white men; they will do with him as they wish. But he can stand torture, and is not afraid of death. He is no coward. Black Hawk is an Indian.

He has done nothing for which an Indian ought to be ashamed. He has fought for his countrymen, the squaws and papooses, against white men, who came, year after year, to cheat them and take away their lands. You know the cause of our making war. It is known to all white men. . . .

An Indian who is as bad as the white men could not live in our nation; he would be put to death and eat up by the wolves. The white men are bad schoolmasters; they carry false looks, and deal in false actions; they smile in the face of the poor Indian to cheat him; they shake them by the hand to gain their confidence, to make them drunk, to deceive them, and ruin our wives. We told them to let us alone, and keep away from us; but they followed on, and beset our paths, and they coiled themselves among us, like the snake. They poisoned us by their touch. We were not safe. We lived in danger. We were becoming like them, hypocrites and liars, adulterers, lazy drones, all talkers, and no workers.

We looked up the Great Spirit. We went to our great father. We were encouraged. His great council gave us fair words and big promises; but we got no satisfaction. . . .

We called a great council, and built a large fire. The spirit of our fathers arose and spoke to us to avenge our wrongs or die. We all spoke before the council fire. It was warm and pleasant. We set up the war-whoop, and dug up the toma-hawk; our knives were ready, and the heart of Black Hawk swelled high in his bosom, when he led his warriors to battle. He is satisfied. He will go to the world of spirits contented. He has done his duty. His father will meet him there, and commend him.

Black Hawk is a true Indian, and disdains to cry like a woman. He feels for his wife, his children and friends. But he does not care for himself. He cares for his nation and the Indi-ans. They will suffer. He laments their fate. The white men do not scalp the head; but they do worse—they poison the heart. . . .

Farewell, my nation! Black Hawk tried to save you, and avenge your wrongs. He drank the blood of some of the whites. He has been taken prisoner, and his plans are stopped. He can do no more. He is near his end. His sun is setting, and he will rise no more. Farewell to Black Hawk.

Sam Houston

"Remember the Alamo!"

San Jacinto, Texas
April 19, 1836

Sam Houston became commander in chief of the Texas revolutionary army in 1836, when Mexico angered American settlers by sending troops to control the territory and by denying Texas self-government. About to fight General Santa Anna's Mexican army at San Jacinto, Houston exhorted his men at length to remember the Alamo and Goliad, two massacres of Texas troops by Mexican forces. Fired to victory by their leader's eloquence, they took "Remember the Alamo!" as their battle cry, and the outnumbered men won the battle that established the freedom of Texas from Mexico. Only fragments remain of the speech, reconstructed from the recollections of those who fought.

☆ ☆

Victory is certain! Trust in God and fear not! The victims of the Alamo and the names of those who were murdered at Goliad cry out for vengeance. Remember the Alamo! Remember Goliad!

Other soldiers recalled

Remember the Alamo! Remember Goliad! Victory or death! [but] there will be no defeat! Victory is as certain as God reigns. I feel the inspiration in every fiber of my being. Trust in the God of the just and fear not!

☆

Elijah Lovejoy

In Defense of a Free Press

Alton, Illinois
November 3, 1837

Elijah Lovejoy was a white abolitionist newspaperman and publisher of the Alton
Observer *in Alton, Illinois. He was driven from state to state by pro-slavery mobs
that destroyed his printing presses three times. At a town meeting of officials and
citizens, Lovejoy passionately defended his rights of free speech and a free press, and
proclaimed his decision to remain in Alton. Four days later he was killed by a mob
while physically defending a new printing press that had arrived only hours before.
His death outraged the American public and gave further impetus to the anti-
slavery movement.*

☆ ☆

Mr. Chairman—it is not true, as has been charged upon me,
that I hold in contempt the feelings and sentiments of this
community, in reference to [slavery,] the question which is now
agitating it. I respect and appreciate the feelings and opinions
of my fellow-citizens, and it is one of the most painful and
unpleasant duties of my life, that I am called upon to act in
opposition to them. If you suppose, sir, that I have published
sentiments contrary to those generally held in this community,
because I delighted in differing from them, or in occasioning a
disturbance, you have entirely misapprehended me.

But, sir, while I value the good opinion of my fellow-citizens,
as highly as any one, I may be permitted to say, that I am governed by higher considerations than either the favour or the
fear of man. I am impelled to the course I have taken, because
I fear God. As I shall answer it to my God in the great day, I
dare not abandon my sentiments [against slavery], or cease in
all proper ways to propagate them.

I, Mr. Chairman, have not desired, or asked any *compromise.*
I have asked for nothing but to be protected in my rights as a

51

citizen—rights which God has given me, and which are guaranteed to me by the constitution of my country. Have I, sir, been guilty of any infraction of the laws? Whose good name have I injured? When and where have I published any thing injurious to the reputation of Alton? . . .

But if I have been guilty of no violation of law, why am I hunted up and down continually like a partridge upon the mountains? Why am I threatened with the *tar-barrel*? Why am I waylaid every day, and from night to night, and my life in jeopardy every hour?

You have, sir, made up, as the lawyers say, a false issue; there are not two parties between whom there can be a *compromise*. I plant myself, sir, down on my unquestionable *rights*, and the question to be decided is, whether I shall be protected in the exercise and enjoyment of those rights—*that is the question, sir*;—whether my property shall be protected, whether I shall be suffered to go home to my family at night without being assailed, and threatened with tar and feathers, and assassination; . . . *that sir, is the question.*

I have no personal fears. Not that I feel able to contest the matter with the whole community, I know perfectly well I am not. I know, sir, that you can tar and feather me, hang me up, or put me into the Mississippi, without the least difficulty. But what then? Where shall I go? I have been made to feel that if I am not safe at Alton, I shall not be safe any where. I recently visited St. Charles to bring home my family, and was torn from their frantic embrace by a mob. I have been beset night and day at Alton. And now if I leave here and go elsewhere, violence may overtake me in my retreat, and I have no more claim upon the protection of any other community than I have upon this; and I have concluded, after consultation with my friends, and earnestly seeking counsel of God, to *remain at Alton*, and here to insist on protection in the exercise of my rights. If the civil authorities refuse to protect me, I must look to God; and if I die, I have determined to make my grave in Alton.

Angelina Grimke

"What Has the North to Do with Slavery?"

Philadelphia, Pennsylvania
May 16, 1838

Angelina Grimke came from a wealthy Charleston, South Carolina, slaveholding family. After she moved north and became a Quaker, Grimke began to lecture against slavery and for women's rights in an era when women were not often welcomed on the lecture platform or pulpit. A powerful orator, she was convinced women had the influence to end slavery in the United States, as they had in England. When she addressed the National Anti-Slavery Convention, a pro-slavery mob stormed Pennsylvania Hall as she spoke, rattling doors and breaking windows. They burned the building down a few days later.

☆ ☆

Do you ask, "What has the North to do with slavery?" Hear it, hear it! Those voices without tell us that the spirit of slavery is *here* and has been roused to wrath by our conventions; for surely liberty would not foam and tear herself with rage, because her friends are multiplied daily, and meetings are held in quick succession to set forth her virtues and extend her peaceful kingdom. This opposition shows that slavery has done its deadliest work in the hearts of our citizens.

Do you ask, then, "What has the North to do?" I answer, cast out first the spirit of slavery from your own hearts, and then lend your aid to convert the South. . . . The great men of this country will not do this work; the church will never do it. A desire to please the world, to keep the favor of all parties and of all conditions, makes them dumb on this and every other unpopular subject.

As a Southerner, I feel that it is my duty to stand up here tonight and bear testimony against slavery. I have seen it! I have seen it! I know it has horrors that can never be described.

I was brought up under its wing. I witnessed for many years its demoralizing influences and its destructiveness to human happiness. I have never seen a happy slave. I have seen him dance in his chains, it is true, but he was not happy. There is a wide difference between happiness and mirth. Man cannot enjoy happiness while his manhood is destroyed. Slaves, however, may be, and sometimes are mirthful. When hope is extinguished, they say, "Let us eat and drink, for tomorrow we die."

What is a mob? What would the breaking of every window be? What would the leveling of this hall be? Any evidence that we are wrong, or that slavery is a good and wholesome institution? What if the mob should now burst in upon us, break up our meeting, and commit violence upon our persons? Would that be anything compared with what the slaves endure? . . .

We often hear the question asked: "What shall we do?" Here is an opportunity. Every man and every woman present may do something, by showing that we fear not a mob. . . . Let me urge everyone to buy the books written on this subject; read them and lend them to your neighbors. Give your money no longer for things which pander to pride and lust, but aid in scattering "the living coals of truth upon the naked heart of the nation," in circulating appeals to the sympathies of Christians in behalf of the outraged slave. . . .

Women of Philadelphia! allow me as a Southern woman, with much attachment to the land of my birth, to entreat you to come up to this work. Especially, let me urge you to petition. Men may settle this and other questions at the ballot-box, but you have no such right. It is only through petitions that you can reach the legislature. It is, therefore, peculiarly your duty to petition. Do you say, "It does no good!" The South already turns pale at the number sent. They have read the reports of the proceedings of Congress and there have seen that among other petitions were very many from the women of the North on the subject of slavery. . . .

It was remarked in England that women did much to abolish slavery in her colonies. Nor are they now idle. . . . Let the zeal and love, the faith and works of our English sisters quicken ours; that while the slaves continue to suffer, and when they shout for deliverance, we may feel the satisfaction of "having done what we could."

☆

Henry Highland Garnet

The Call to Rebellion

Buffalo, New York
August 15, 1843

Henry Highland Garnet escaped from slavery in Maryland as a nine-year-old child and grew up to become a clergyman in New York. He lectured widely in the United States and abroad, and later he became U.S. minister to Liberia. He was most famous for his address to the 1843 National Negro Convention. The tone of the speech, with its advocacy of violent rebellion, was considered far too militant at the time even for black leaders to accept, and Garnet's resolution was voted down.

☆ ☆

Two hundred and twenty-seven years ago the first of our injured race were brought to the shores of America. They came not with glad spirits to select their homes in the New World. They came not with their own consent, to find an unmolested enjoyment of the blessings of this fruitful soil. . . . They came with broken hearts, from their beloved native land, and were doomed to unrequited toil and deep degradation. Nor did the evil of their bondage end at their emancipation by death. Succeeding generations inherited their chains, and millions have come from eternity into time, and have returned again to the world of spirits, cursed and ruined by American slavery. . . .

Brethren, the time has come when you must act for yourselves. It is an old and true saying that, "if hereditary bondmen would be free, they must themselves strike the blow." . . . Think of the undying glory that hangs around the ancient name of Africa—and forget not that you are native-born American citizens, and as such you are justly entitled to all the rights that are granted to the freest. Think how many tears you have poured out upon the soil which you have cultivated

56

with unrequited toil and enriched with your blood; and then go to your lordly enslavers and tell them plainly, that you *are determined to be free.* . . .

Do this, and forever after cease to toil for the heartless tyrants, who give you no other reward but stripes and abuse. If they then commence work of death, they, and not you, will be responsible for the consequences. You had far better all die—die immediately, than live slaves, and entail your wretchedness upon your posterity. If you would be free in this generation, here is your only hope. However much you and all of us may desire it, there is not much hope of redemption without the shedding of blood. If you must bleed, let it all come at once—rather die freemen than live to be slaves. . . .

Fellowmen! patient sufferers! behold your dearest rights crushed to the earth! See your sons murdered, and your wives, mothers and sisters doomed to prostitution. In the name of the merciful God, and by all that life is worth, let it no longer be a debatable question, whether it is better to choose *liberty* or *death.* . . .

Brethren, arise, arise! Strike for your lives and liberties. Now is the day and the hour. Let every slave throughout the land do this, and the days of slavery are numbered. You cannot be more oppressed than you have been—you cannot suffer greater cruelties than you have already. *Rather die freemen than live to be slaves.* . . .

Let your motto be resistance! *resistance!* RESISTANCE! No oppressed people have ever secured their liberty without resistance. What kind of resistance you had better make you must decide by the circumstances that surround you. . . . Brethren, adieu! Trust in the living God. Labor for the peace of the human race, and remember that you are FOUR MILLIONS!

Lewis Richardson

"My Grave Shall Be Made in Free Soil"

Amherstburg, Canada West (now Ontario)
March 13, 1846

Slaves escaping from the slave states of the United States were only truly free once they reached Canada. Even in the non-slave states of the North, they could be captured and returned to their owners, and the rewards offered for their capture made slave-hunting a business for some people. Lewis Richardson, a fugitive slave owned by Kentucky senator Henry Clay who had escaped in December 1845, gave this stirring speech at an antislavery meeting after crossing the Detroit River into Canada.

☆ ☆

Dear Brethren, I am truly happy to meet with you on British soil, where I am not known by the color of my skin, but where the Government knows me as a man. But I am free from American slavery, after wearing the galling chains on my limbs 53 years, nine of which it has been my unhappy lot to be the slave of Henry Clay. It has been said by some, that Clay's slaves had rather live with him than be free, but I had rather this day have a millstone tied to my neck, and be sunk to the bottom of Detroit river, than to go back to Ashland and be his slave for life. As late as December, 1845, Henry Clay had me stripped and tied up, and one hundred and fifty lashes given me on my naked back: the crime for which I was so abused was, I failed to return home on a visit to see my wife, on Monday morning, before 5 o'clock. My wife was living on another place, three miles from Ashland.

During the nine years living with Mr. Clay, he has not given me a hat nor cap to wear, nor a stitch of bed clothes, except one small coarse blanket. Yet he has said publicly his slaves were "fat and slick!" But I say if they are, it is not because they are so well used by him. They have nothing but coarse bread and meat to eat and not enough of that. They are allowanced every week. For each field hand is allowed one peck of coarse corn meal and meat in proportion, and no vegetables of any kind. Such is the treatment that Henry Clay's slaves receive from him.

I can truly say that I have only one thing to lament over, and that is my bereft wife who is yet in bondage. If I only had her with me I should be happy. Yet think not that I am unhappy. Think not that I regret the choice that I have made. I counted the cost before I started. Before I took leave of my wife, she wept over me, and dressed the wounds on my back caused by the lash. I then gave her the parting hand, and started for Canada.

I expected to be pursued as a felon, as I had been before, and to be hunted as a fox from mountain to cave. I well knew if I continued much longer with Clay, that I should be killed by such floggings and abuse by his cruel overseer in my old age. I wanted to be free before I died—and if I should be caught on the way to Canada and taken back, it could but be death, and I might as well die with the colic as the fever. With these considerations I started for Canada.

Such usage as this caused me to flee from under the American eagle, and take shelter under the British crown. Thanks be to Heaven that I have got here at last: on yonder side of Detroit river, I was recognized as property; but on this side I am on free soil. Hail, Britannia! Shame, America! A Republican despotism, holding three millions of our fellow men in slavery. Oh what a contrast between slavery and liberty! Here I stand erect, without a chain upon my limbs. Redeemed, emancipated, by the generosity of Great Britain.

I now feel as independent as ever Henry Clay felt when he was running for the White House. In fact I feel better. He has been defeated four or five times, and I but once. But he was running for slavery, and I for liberty. I think I have beat him out of sight. Thanks be to God that I am elected to Canada, and if I don't live but one night, I am determined to die on free soil. Let my days be few or many, let me die sooner or later, my grave shall be made in free soil.

Thomas Corwin

Against War with Mexico

U.S. Senate, Washington, D.C.
February 11, 1847

Ohio senator Thomas Corwin was one of many Americans who bitterly opposed the Mexican War. After Texas was annexed, in 1845, President James Polk made clear his interest in obtaining California for the United States, but Mexico would not sell, and the war began. Corwin caused a stir in the senate when he denounced American expansionist intentions in pursuing the war and accurately predicted that the conquests would inflame tensions between North and South over whether territories would enter the Union slave or free. Although his speech was well-regarded, he was the only senator to vote against the war.

☆ ☆

Mr. President: . . . You have overrun half of Mexico—you have exasperated and irritated her people—you claim indemnity for all expenses incurred in doing this mischief, and boldly ask her to give up New Mexico and California. . . .

But, sir, let us see what, as the chairman of the Committee on Foreign Relations explains it, we are to get by the combined processes of conquest and treaty.

What is the territory, Mr. President, which you propose to wrest from Mexico? It is consecrated to the heart of the Mexican by many a well-fought battle with his old Castilian master. His Bunker Hills, and Saratogas, and Yorktowns, are there! The Mexican can say, "There I bled for liberty! and shall I surrender that consecrated home of my affections to the Anglo-Saxon invaders? What do they want with it? They have Texas already. They have possessed themselves of the territory between the Nueces and the Rio Grande. What else do they want? To what shall I point my children as memorials of that independence which I bequeath to them when those battlefields shall have passed from my possession?"

Sir, had one come and demanded Bunker Hill of the people of Massachusetts, had England's lion ever showed himself there, is there a man over thirteen, and under ninety, who would not have been ready to meet him—is there a river on this continent that would not have run red with blood—is there a field but would have been piled high with the unburied bones of slaughtered Americans before these consecrated battlefields of liberty should have been wrested from us? But this same American goes into a sister republic, and says to poor, weak Mexico, "Give up your territory—you are unworthy to possess it—I have got one-half already—all I ask you is to give up the other!" . . .

Sir, look at this pretense of want of room. With twenty millions of people, you have about one thousand millions of acres of land, inviting settlement by every conceivable argument—bringing them down to a quarter of a dollar an acre, and allowing every man to squat where he pleases. But the Senator from Michigan says we will be two hundred millions in a few years, and we want room. If I were a Mexican I would tell you, "Have you not room in your own country to bury your dead men? If you come into mine we will greet you with bloody hands, and welcome you to hospitable graves."

Why, says the chairman of this Committee of Foreign Relations, it is the most reasonable thing in the world! We ought to have the Bay of San Francisco. Why? Because it is the best harbor on the Pacific! It has been my fortune, Mr. President, to have practiced a good deal in criminal courts in the course of my life, but I never yet heard a thief, arraigned for stealing a horse, plead that it was the best horse that he could find in the country! We want California. What for? "Why," says the Senator from Michigan, "we will have it;" and the Senator from South Carolina, with a very mistaken view, I think, of policy, says, "You can't keep our people from going there." I don't desire to prevent them. Let them go and seek their happiness in whatever country or clime it pleases them.

All I ask of them is, not to require this Government to protect them with that banner consecrated to war waged for principles—eternal, enduring truth. Sir, it is not meet that our old flag should throw its protecting folds over expeditions for lucre or for land. But you still say, you want room for your people. This has been the plea of every robber-chief from Nimrod to the present hour. I dare say, when Tamerlane descended from his throne built of seventy thousand human skulls, and marched his ferocious battalions to further slaughter, I dare say he said, "I want room." . . . Alexander, too, the mighty "Macedonian madman," when he wandered with his Greeks to the plains of India, . . . was, no doubt, in quest of some California there. . . .

Whatever we may say to-day, or whatever we may write in our books, the stern tribunal of history will review it all, detect falsehood, and bring us to judgment before that posterity which shall bless or curse us, as we may act *now*, wisely or otherwise.

Frederick Douglass

"If I Had a Country, I Should Be a Patriot"

Syracuse, New York
September 24, 1847

As a slave in Maryland, Frederick Douglass taught himself to read and write and studied carefully the first book be bought himself, a children's book of speeches. He escaped to New Bedford, Massachusetts, in 1838 at the age of 21 and later sailed to Britain to avoid recapture. There he found many friends at antislavery societies and made speeches to enlist support against slavery in the United States. When English friends paid 150 pounds for his freedom, he was able to return and gave this address on a slave's view of patriotism on his first speaking tour after his arrival home.

☆ ☆

Ours is a glorious land, and from across the Atlantic we welcome those who are stricken by the storms of despotism. Yet the damning fact remains, there is not a rood of earth under the stars and the eagle on your flag, where a man of my complexion can stand free. There is no mountain so high, no plain so extensive, no spot so sacred, that it can secure to me the right of liberty. Wherever waves the star-spangled banner there the bondman may be arrested and hurried back to the jaws of Slavery. This is your "land of the free," your "home of the brave." . . .

I never knew what freedom was till I got beyond the limits of the American eagle. When I first rested my head on a British Island, I felt that the eagle might scream, but from its talons and beak I was free, at least for a time. . . .

I know this kind of talk is not agreeable to what are called patriots. Indeed some have called me a traitor. . . . Two things are necessary to make a traitor. One is, he shall have a country. I believe if I had a country, I should be a patriot. I think I have all the feelings necessary—all the moral material, to say nothing about the intellectual. I do not know that I ever felt the emotion, but sometimes thought I had a glimpse of it. When I have been delighted with the little brook that passes by the cottage in which I was born, with the woods and the fertile fields, I felt a sort of glow which I suspect resembles a little what they call patriotism. I can look with some admiration on your wide lakes, your fertile fields, your enterprise, your industry, your many lovely institutions. I can read with pleasure your Constitution to establish justice and secure the blessings of liberty to posterity. Those are precious sayings to my mind.

But when I remember that the blood of four sisters and one brother is making fat the soil of Maryland and Virginia—when I remember that an aged grandmother . . . reared twelve children for the Southern [slave] market, and these one after another . . . were torn from her bosom—when I remember that when she became too much racked for toil, she was turned out by a professed Christian master to grope her way in the darkness of old age, literally to die with none to help her, and the institutions of this country sanctioning and sanctifying this crime, I have no words of eulogy, I have no patriotism. How can I love a country where the blood of my own blood, the flesh of my own flesh, is now toiling under the lash? . . .

No, I make no pretension to patriotism. So long as my voice can be heard on this or the other side of the Atlantic, I will hold up America to the lightning scorn of moral indignation. In doing this, I shall feel myself discharging the duty of a true patriot; for he is a lover of his country who rebukes and does not excuse its sins.

☆

Henry Clay

A Call for a Measure of Compromise

U.S. Senate, Washington, D.C.
July 22, 1850

Called the "Great Compromiser," Henry Clay was a senator from Kentucky and three times the Speaker of the House. He ran for president many times but was never elected. In 1850, when the northern and southern states were bitterly opposed over the spread of slavery into new territories, Clay proposed a compromise with the aim of preventing the breakup of the Union. But the measure he introduced in the Senate with the support of Daniel Webster (now called the Compromise of 1850) only succeeded in delaying the Civil War for another ten years.

☆ ☆

It has been objected against this measure that it is a compromise. It has been said that it is a compromise of principle, or of a principle. Mr. President, what is a compromise? It is a work of mutual concession—an agreement in which there are reciprocal stipulations—a work in which, for the sake of peace and concord, one party abates his extreme demands in consideration of an abatement of extreme demands by the other party: it is a measure of mutual concession—a measure of mutual sacrifice. . . .

The responsibility of this great measure passes from the hands of the committee, and from my hands. They know, and I know, that it is an awful and tremendous responsibility. I hope that you will meet it with a just conception and a true appreciation of its magnitude. . . . I believe from the bottom of my soul that the measure is the reunion of this Union. . . .

Let us look to our country and our cause, elevate ourselves to the dignity of pure and disinterested patriots, and save our country from all impending dangers. What if, in the march of this nation to greatness and power, we should be buried beneath the wheels that propel it onward! What are we—what

67

is any man—worth who is not ready and willing to sacrifice himself for the benefit of his country when it is necessary?

I call upon all the South. Sir, we have had hard words, bitter words, bitter thoughts, unpleasant feelings toward each other in the progress of this great measure. Let us forget them. Let us sacrifice these feelings. Let us go to the altar of our country and swear, as the oath was taken of old, that we will stand by her; that we will support her; that we will uphold her Constitution; that we will preserve her Union; and that we will pass this great, comprehensive, and healing system of measures, which will hush all the jarring elements and bring peace and tranquillity to our homes.

Let me, Mr. President, in conclusion, say that the most disastrous consequences would occur, in my opinion, were we to go home, doing nothing to satisfy and tranquillize the country upon these great questions. What will be the judgment of mankind? . . . Will not all the monarchs of the Old World pronounce our glorious Republic a disgraceful failure? . . . We shall stand condemned in our own consciences, by our own constituents, and by our own country. The measure may be defeated. I have been aware that its passage for many days was not absolutely certain. From the first to the last, I hoped and believed it would pass, because from the first to the last I believed it was founded on the principles of just and righteous concession, of mutual conciliation. I believe that it deals unjustly by no part of the Republic; that it saves their honor and, as far as it is dependent upon Congress, saves the interests of all quarters of the country. . . .

But, if defeated, it will be a triumph of ultraism and impracticability—a triumph of a most extraordinary conjunction of extremes; a victory won by abolitionism; a victory achieved by free-soilism; a victory of discord and agitation over peace and tranquillity; and I pray to Almighty God that it may not, in consequence of the inauspicious result, lead to the most unhappy and disastrous consequences to our beloved country.

Sojourner Truth

"If You Have Woman's Rights, Give Them to Her"

Akron, Ohio
May 29, 1851

Sojourner Truth was named Isabella when she was born in 1797 as a slave belonging to a Dutch family in New York State. Freed in 1828, she changed her name and traveled the country preaching against slavery and for women's rights. Her colorful language and good common sense made her a powerful speaker. She is best remembered today for a speech she probably never gave at the 1851 Ohio Woman's Rights Convention. Historians have concluded that the popular version "Ain't I a Woman?" was written twelve years afterward by the convention's organizer and is not as authentic as the one reproduced here, which was taken down on the day of the actual speech by Marius Robinson, recording secretary for the convention.

☆ ☆

I am a woman's rights.

I have as much muscle as any man, and can do as much work as any man. I have plowed and reaped and husked and chopped and mowed, and can any man do more than that? . . .

I have heard much about the sexes being equal. . . . As for intellect all I can say is, if a woman [has] a pint and man a quart—why can't she have her little pint full? You need not be afraid to give us our rights for fear we will take too much, for we can't take more than our pint'll hold.

The poor men seem to be all in confusion, and don't know what to do. Why children, if you have woman's rights, give [them] to her and you will feel better. You will have your own rights, and they won't be so much trouble.

I can't read, but I can hear. I have heard the Bible and have learned that Eve caused man to sin. Well, if woman upset the world, do give her a chance to set it right side up again. The lady has spoken about Jesus, how he never spurned woman from him, and she was right. . . . And how came Jesus into the world? Through God who created him and woman who bore him. Man, where is your part? . . .

But man is in a tight place, the poor slave is on him, woman is coming on him, and he is surely between a hawk and a buzzard.

Frederick Douglass

"What to the American Slave Is Your Fourth of July?"

Rochester, New York
July 5, 1852

In recognition of the fact that they were not free, American slaves held their observance of Independence Day on the fifth of July rather than the fourth. Invited to give the holiday address in 1852, Frederick Douglass rejected Independence Day as a hypocrisy to the slave. By this time, he had transcended his birth in slavery and his lack of a formal education to become one of America's greatest orators, a confidant of President Lincoln, and U.S. minister to Haiti.

☆ ☆

Fellow citizens, pardon me, allow me to ask, Why am I called upon to speak here today? What have I, or those I represent, to do with your national independence? Are the great principles of political freedom and of natural justice, embodied in that Declaration of Independence, extended to us? . . .

What, to the American slave, is your Fourth of July? I answer: a day that reveals to him, more than all other days in the year, the gross injustice and cruelty to which he is the constant victim. To him, your celebration is a sham; your boasted liberty, an unholy license; your national greatness, swelling vanity; your sounds of rejoicing are empty and heartless; your denunciation of tyrants, brass-fronted impudence; your shouts of liberty and equality, hollow mockery; your prayers and hymns, your sermons and thanksgivings, with all your religious parade and solemnity, are, to him, mere bombast, fraud, deception, impiety, and hypocrisy—a thin veil to cover up crimes which would disgrace a nation of savages. There is

71

not a nation on the earth guilty of practices more shocking and bloody than are the people of the United States at this very hour.

Go where you may, search where you will, roam through all the monarchies and despotisms of the Old World, travel through South America, search out every abuse, and when you have found the last, lay your facts by the side of the every-day practices of this nation, and you will say with me that, for revolting barbarity and shameless hypocrisy, America reigns without a rival.

Ralph Waldo Emerson

On the Fugitive Slave Law

New York City
March 7, 1854

The thinker, preacher, and poet of Boston, Ralph Waldo Emerson made his living from lecturing. Not naturally a powerful orator, he derived his success instead from his message of individualism and the greatness of God within each person. He was drawn into the abolitionist movement by his horror at the Compromise of 1850, which included the Fugitive Slave Law, a deal between the free states of the North and the slave states of the South that required the return of escaped slaves even from states where slavery was prohibited.

☆ ☆

I have lived all my life without suffering any known inconvenience from American slavery. I never saw it; I never heard the whip; I never felt the check on my free speech and action until the other day, when Mr. Webster, by his personal influence, brought the Fugitive Slave Law on the country.

I say Mr. Webster, for though the bill was not his, it is yet notorious that he was the life and soul of it, that he gave it all he had. It cost him his life, and under the shadow of his great name inferior men sheltered themselves, threw their ballots for it and made the law.

I say inferior men. There were all sorts of what are called brilliant men, accomplished men, men of high station, a President of the United States, senators, men of eloquent speech, but men without self-respect, without character; and it was strange to see that office, age, fame, talent, even a repute for honesty all count for nothing.

They had no opinions, they had no memory for what they had been saying like the Lord's Prayer all their lifetime: they were only looking to what their great Captain did. If he jumped, they jumped; if he stood on his head, they did. . . .

I said I had never in my life up to this time suffered from the slave institution. Slavery in Virginia or Carolina was like slavery in Africa or the Fijis for me. There was an old Fugitive Law, but it had become, or was fast becoming, a dead letter, and, by the genius and laws of Massachusetts, inoperative. The new bill made it operative, required me to hunt slaves, and it found citizens in Massachusetts willing to act as judges and captors. . . .

It showed that the old religion and the sense of the right had faded and gone out; that while we reckoned ourselves a highly cultivated nation, our bellies had run away with our brains, and the principles of culture and progress did not exist.

For I suppose that liberty is an accurate index, in men and nations, of general progress. The theory of personal liberty must always appeal to the most refined communities and to the men of the rarest perception and of delicate moral sense. For there are rights which rest on the finest sense of justice. . . .

To make good the cause of freedom, you must draw off from all foolish trust in others. You must be citadels and warriors yourselves, declarations of independence, the charter, the battle, and the victory. . . .

He only who is able to stand alone is qualified for society. And that I understand to be the end for which a soul exists in this world—to be himself the counterbalance of all falsehood and all wrong. . . .

Now at last we are disenchanted and shall have no more false hopes. I respect the Anti-Slavery Society. It is the Cassandra that has foretold all that has befallen, fact for fact, years ago; foretold all, and no man laid it to heart. It seemed, as the Turks say, "Fate makes that a man should not believe his own eyes." But the Fugitive Law did much to unglue the eyes of men, and now the Nebraska Bill leaves us staring. The Anti-Slavery Society will add many members this year. The

Whig Party will join it; the Democrats will join it. The population of the free states will join it. I doubt not, at last, the slave states will join it.

But be that sooner or later, and whoever comes or stays away, I hope we have reached the end of our unbelief, have come to a belief that there is a divine Providence in the world which will not save us but through our own cooperation.

Seattle, Duwamish Chief

"We Will Dwell Apart and in Peace"

Seattle, Washington Territory
Probably March 1854

Governor Isaac Stevens arrived in Washington Territory in late 1853 to survey for the transcontinental railroad and make proposals to the Indians for the sale of their lands. Meeting with Stevens, Chief Seattle of the Duwamish delivered an eloquent speech on the future of his tribe and the spiritual life of the Indian. Seattle agreed to Stevens's proposals and referred to President Franklin Pierce as "Washington." There has been disagreement among scholars over the authenticity of the speech, as it was set down by a witness, Henry Smith, many years later, and rewritten by others in the following century. This version is the earliest known, written by Smith and printed in the Seattle Sunday Star *of October 29, 1887.*

☆ ☆

My words are like the stars that never set. What Seattle says the great chief, Washington, can rely upon, with as much certainty as our pale-face brothers can rely upon the return of the seasons. The son of the white chief says his father sends us greetings of friendship and good-will. This is kind, for we know he has little need of our friendship in return, because his people are many. They are like the grass that covers the vast prairies, while my people are few, and resemble the scattering trees of a wind-swept plain.

The great, and I presume also good, white chief sends us word that he wants to buy our lands but is willing to allow us to reserve enough to live on comfortably. This indeed appears generous, for the red man no longer has rights that he need respect, and the offer may be wise, also, for we are no longer in need of a great country. There was a time when our people covered the whole land as the waves of a wind-ruffled sea cover its shell-paved floor. But that time has long since passed away with the greatness of tribes now almost forgotten. I will not mourn over our untimely decay, nor reproach my pale-face brothers with hastening it, for we, too, may have been somewhat to blame.

When our young men grow angry at some real or imaginary wrong, and disfigure their faces with black paint, their hearts, also, are disfigured and turn black, and then their cruelty is relentless and knows no bounds, and our old men are not able to restrain them. But let us hope that hostilities between the red-man and his pale-face brothers may never return. We would have everything to lose and nothing to gain.

No, we are two distinct races and must ever remain so. There is little in common between us. The ashes of our ancestors are sacred and their final resting place is hallowed ground, while you wander away from the tombs of your fathers seemingly without regret.

Your religion was written on tables of stone by the iron finger of an angry God, lest you might forget it. The red man could never remember nor comprehend it.

Our religion is the traditions of our ancestors, the dreams of our old men, given them by the great Spirit, and the visions of our sachems, and is written in the hearts of our people. . . . Day and night cannot dwell together. The red man has ever fled the approach of the white man, as the changing mists on the mountain side flee before the blazing morning sun.

However, your proposition seems a just one, and I think my folks will accept it and will retire to the reservation you offer them, and we will dwell apart and in peace, for the words of the great white chief seem to be the voice of nature speaking to my people out of the thick darkness that is fast gathering around them like a dense fog floating inward from a midnight sea.

It matters but little where we pass the remainder of our days. They are not many. The Indian's night promises to be dark. No bright star hovers about the horizon. . . . A few more moons, a few more winters and not one of all the mighty hosts that once filled this broad land or that now roam in

fragmentary bands through these vast solitudes will remain to
weep over the tombs of a people once as powerful and as
hopeful as your own. . . .

We will ponder your proposition, and when we have
decided we will tell you. But should we accept it, I here and
now make this the first condition: That we will not be denied
the privilege, without molestation, of visiting at will the
graves of our ancestors and friends. Every part of this country
is sacred to my people. Every hillside, every valley, every plain
and grove has been hallowed by some fond memory or some
sad experience of my tribe. Even the rocks that seem to lie
dumb as they swelter in the sun along the silent seashore in
solemn grandeur thrill with memories of past events connected with the fate of my people, and the very dust under
your feet responds more lovingly to our footsteps than to
yours, because it is the ashes of our ancestors, and our bare
feet are conscious of the sympathetic touch, for the soil is rich
with the life of our kindred.

The sable braves, and fond mothers, and glad-hearted
maidens, and the little children who lived and rejoiced here,
and whose very names are now forgotten, still love these solitudes, and their deep fastnesses at eventide grow shadowy
with the presence of dusky spirits.

And when the last red man shall have perished from the
earth and his memory among white men shall have become a
myth, these shores shall swarm with the invisible dead of my
tribe, and when your children's children shall think themselves alone in the field, the store, the shop, upon the highway
or in the silence of the woods they will not be alone. In all the
earth there is no place dedicated to solitude. At night when
the streets of your cities and villages shall be silent, and you
think them deserted, they will throng with the returning hosts
that once filled and still love this beautiful land.

The white man will never be alone. Let him be just and deal
kindly with my people, for the dead are not altogether powerless.

Lucy Stone

"A Disappointed Woman"

Cincinnati, Ohio
October 17, 1855

Lucy Stone, from Massachusetts, was one of the first American women to attend college and to keep her maiden name after marriage (she married Henry Blackwell but called herself Mrs. Stone). She lectured widely on women's rights and for the abolition of slavery. She was a superb orator, and at the 1855 National Woman's Rights Convention she cleverly took the lead from a male speaker who had just referred to the women's rights movement as being the work of "a few disappointed women."

☆ ☆

The last speaker alluded to this movement as being that of a few disappointed women.

From the first years to which my memory stretches, I have been a disappointed woman. When, with my brothers, I reached forth after the sources of knowledge, I was reproved with "It isn't fit for you; it doesn't belong to women." Then there was but one college in the world where women were admitted, and that was in Brazil. I would have found my way there, but by the time I was prepared to go, one was opened in the young State of Ohio—the first in the United States where women and Negroes could enjoy opportunities with white men.

I was disappointed when I came to seek a profession worthy an immortal being—every employment was closed to me, except those of the teacher, the seamstress, and the housekeeper. In education, in marriage, in religion, in everything, disappointment is the lot of woman.

It shall be the business of my life to deepen this disappointment in every woman's heart until she bows down to it no longer. I wish that women, instead of being walking show-cases, instead of begging of their fathers and brothers the latest and gayest new bonnet, would ask of them their rights.

The question of Woman's Rights is a practical one. The notion has prevailed that it was only an ephemeral idea; that it was but women claiming the right to smoke cigars in the streets, and to frequent bar-rooms. Others have supposed it a question of comparative intellect; others still, of sphere. Too much has already been said and written about woman's sphere. Trace all the doctrines to their source and they will be found to have no basis except in the usages and prejudices of the age. This is seen in the fact that what is tolerated in woman in one country is not tolerated in another. In this country women may hold prayer-meetings, etc., but in Mohammedan countries it is written upon their mosques, "Women and dogs, and other impure animals, are not permitted to enter."

Wendell Phillips says, "The best and greatest thing one is capable of doing, that is his sphere." I have confidence in the Father to believe that when He gives us the capacity to do anything He does not make a blunder. Leave women, then, to find their sphere. And do not tell us before we are born even, that our province is to cook dinners, darn stockings, and sew on buttons.

☆

Abraham Lincoln

"A House Divided"

Springfield, Illinois
June 16, 1858

Abraham Lincoln, then a lawyer in Illinois, was nominated by the Republican Party in 1858 to run for the office of U.S. senator against the Democrat Stephen Douglas. In his speech at the close of the state convention, he paraphrased the Bible in describing the nation as "a house divided" on the issue of slavery, and he predicted that the institution of slavery would destroy the Union if permitted to continue its divisive course. Lincoln lost the election to Douglas after the debates that followed, but by then he had achieved a national prominence which would allow him to win the presidency in 1860.

☆ ☆

Mr. President and gentlemen of the convention: If we could first know where we are, and whither we are tending, we could better judge what to do, and how to do it.

We are now far into the fifth year since a policy was initiated with the avowed object, and confident promise, of putting an end to slavery agitation. Under the operation of that policy, that agitation not only has not ceased, but has constantly augmented. In my opinion, it will not cease until a crisis shall have been reached and passed. "A house divided against itself cannot stand." I believe this government cannot endure permanently half slave and half free. I do not expect the Union to be dissolved; I do not expect the house to fall; but I do expect that it will cease to be divided. It will become all one thing, or all the other. Either the opponents of slavery will arrest the further spread of it, and place it where the public mind shall rest in the belief that it is in the course of ultimate extinction; or its advocates will push it forward till it shall become alike lawful in all the States, old as well as new, North as well as South.

Have we no tendency to the latter condition? Let anyone who doubts carefully contemplate that now almost complete legal combination-piece of machinery, so to speak—compounded of the Nebraska doctrine and the Dred Scott decision. . . . Put this and that together, and we have another nice little niche, which we may, ere long, see filled with another Supreme Court decision, declaring that the constitution of the United States does not permit a State to exclude slavery from its limits. And this may especially be expected if the doctrine of "care not whether slavery be voted down or voted up," shall gain upon the public mind sufficiently to give promise that such a decision can be maintained when made.

Such a decision is all that slavery now lacks of being alike lawful in all the States. Welcome or unwelcome, such decision is probably coming, and will soon be upon us, unless the power of the present political dynasty shall be met and overthrown. We shall lie down pleasantly dreaming that the people of Missouri are on the verge of making their State free, and we shall awake to the reality, instead, that the Supreme Court has made Illinois a slave State. . . .

Our cause, then, must be intrusted to, and conducted by its own undoubted friends—those whose hands are free, whose hearts are in the work—who do care for the result. Two years ago the Republicans of the nation mustered over thirteen hundred thousand strong. We did this under the single impulse of resistance to a common danger. With every external circumstance against us, of strange, discordant, and even hostile elements, we gathered from the four winds, and formed and fought the battle through under the constant hot fire of a disciplined, proud, and pampered enemy. Did we brave all then, to falter now?—now, when that same enemy is wavering, dissevered, and belligerent! The result is not doubtful. We shall not fail—if we stand firm, we shall not fail. Wise counsels may accelerate, or mistakes delay it; but, sooner or later, the victory is sure to come.

Stephen Douglas

Sixth Lincoln-Douglas Debate

Quincy, Illinois
October 13, 1858

Stephen Douglas had been U.S. senator from Illinois for twelve years when he ran for reelection against Abraham Lincoln. The Lincoln-Douglas campaign debates were held in seven Illinois cities from late summer through fall of 1858. Douglas, a Democrat, was an ardent supporter of states' rights, Western expansion, and popular sovereignty, the principle that each new state or territory had the right to accept or exclude slavery. Lincoln's persistent theme was the moral issue of slavery and the need to stop it. Lincoln won the vote of the people, but Douglas was elected by the legislature. The format of the debates, with moral issues as topics, is still used today by high school debate societies.

☆ ☆

Mr. Lincoln tells you that I will not argue the question whether slavery is right or wrong. I tell you why I will not do it. I hold that under the Constitution of the United States, each State of this Union has a right to do as it pleases on the subject of slavery. . . .

I will stand by that great principle, no matter who may desert it. I intend to stand by it for the purpose of preserving peace between the North and the South, the free and the slave States. If each State will only agree to mind its own business, and let its neighbors alone, there will be peace forever between us.

We in Illinois tried slavery when a Territory, and found it was not good for us in this climate, and with our surroundings, and hence we abolished it. We then adopted a free State Constitution, as we had a right to do. In this State we have declared that a Negro shall not be a citizen, and we have also declared that he shall not be a slave. We had a right to adopt that policy. Missouri has just as good a right to adopt the other policy.

I am now speaking of rights under the Constitution, and not of moral or religious rights. I do not discuss the morals of the people of Missouri, but let them settle that matter for themselves. I hold that the people of the slaveholding States are civilized men as well as ourselves; that they bear consciences as well as we, and that they are accountable to God and their posterity, and not to us. It is for them to decide, therefore, the moral and religious right of the slavery question for themselves within their own limits. I assert that they had as much right under the Constitution to adopt the system of policy which they have as we had to adopt ours. So it is with every other State in this Union.

Let each State stand firmly by that great Constitutional right, let each State mind its own business and let its neighbors alone, and there will be no trouble on this question. If we will stand by that principle, then Mr. Lincoln will find that this Republic can exist forever divided into free and slave States, as our fathers made it and the people of each State have decided. Stand by that great principle, and we can go on as we have done, increasing in wealth, in population, in power, and in all the elements of greatness, until we shall be the admiration and terror of the world. We can go on and enlarge as our population increases, and requires more room, until we make this continent one ocean-bound republic.

Under that principle the United States can perform that great mission, that destiny, which Providence has marked out for us.

John Brown

To the Court after Sentencing

Charles Town, Virginia (now West Virginia)
November 2, 1859

John Brown's passion for abolition drove him to violent acts that included involvement in the murder of five pro-slavery Kansas men. On October 16, 1859, he and a band of followers attacked the federal arsenal in Harper's Ferry, Virginia (now West Virginia), hoping to arm local slaves. He was captured after a battle during which ten men were killed. While many denounced Brown's methods, his speech after being sentenced to hang for treason made him a revered figure among many abolitionists and African Americans.

☆ ☆

I have, may it please the court, a few words to say. In the first place, I deny everything but what I have all along admitted: of a design on my part to free slaves. I intended certainly to have made a clean thing of that matter, as I did last winter, when I went into Missouri and there took slaves without the snapping of a gun on either side, moving them through the country, and finally leaving them in Canada. I designed to have done the same thing again on a larger scale. That was all I intended. I never did intend murder, or treason, or the destruction of property, or to excite or incite slaves to rebellion, or to make insurrection.

I have another objection, and that is that it is unjust that I should suffer such a penalty. Had I interfered in the manner which I admit, and which I admit has been fairly proved—for I admire the truthfulness and candor of the greater portion of the witnesses who have testified in this case—had I so interfered in behalf of the rich, the powerful, the intelligent, the so-called great, or in behalf of any of their friends, either father, mother, brother, sister, wife, or children, or any of that class, and suffered and sacrificed what I have in this interference, it would have been all right. Every man in this court would have deemed it an act worthy of reward rather than punishment.

This court acknowledges, too, as I suppose, the validity of the law of God. I see a book kissed, which I suppose to be the Bible, or at least the New Testament, which teaches me that all things whatsoever I would that men should do to me, I should do even so to them. It teaches me, further, to remember them that are in bonds as bound with them. I endeavored to act up to the instruction. I say I am yet too young to understand that God is any respecter of persons. I believe that to have interfered as I have done, as I have always freely admitted I have done, in behalf of His despised poor, I did not wrong but right. Now, if it is deemed necessary that I should forfeit my life for the furtherance of the ends of justice, and mingle my blood further with the blood of my children and with the blood of millions in this slave country whose rights are disregarded by wicked, cruel, and unjust enactments, I say let it be done.

William Lloyd Garrison

On the Death of John Brown

Boston, Massachusetts
December 2, 1859

William Lloyd Garrison of Massachusetts was the fiery abolitionist publisher of the antislavery newspaper The Liberator. *He was unwilling to compromise on slavery and even supported secession from the Union if it would rid the North of the slave-holding states of the South. Garrison organized numerous antislavery societies to sponsor abolitionist speakers, who were often mobbed and sparked riots. The day of the execution of John Brown, the abolitionist martyr who had attacked the federal arsenal at Harpers Ferry, Garrison delivered a stinging attack on slavery.*

☆ ☆

God forbid that we should any longer continue the accomplices of thieves and robbers, of men-stealers and women-whippers! We must join together in the name of freedom. As for the Union—where is it and what is it? In one-half of it no man can exercise freedom of speech or the press—no man can utter the words of Washington, of Jefferson, of Patrick Henry—except at the peril of his life; and Northern men are everywhere hunted and driven from the South if they are supposed to cherish the sentiment of freedom in their bosoms.

We are living under an awful despotism—that of a brutal slave oligarchy. And they threaten to leave us if we do not continue to do their evil work, as we have hitherto done it, and go down in the dust before them! Would to heaven they would go! It would only be the paupers clearing out from the town, would it not? But, no, they do not mean to go; they mean to cling to you, and they mean to subdue you.

But will you be subdued? I tell you our work is the dissolution of this slavery-cursed Union, if we would have a fragment of our liberties left to us! Surely between freemen, who believe in exact justice and impartial liberty, and slaveholders, who are for cleaning down all human rights at a blow, it is not possible there should be any Union whatever. "How can two walk together except they be agreed?" The slaveholder with his hands dripping in blood—will I make a compact with him? The man who plunders cradles—will I say to him, "Brother, let us walk together in unity"? . . .

What union has freedom with slavery? Let us tell the inexorable and remorseless tyrants of the South that their conditions hitherto imposed upon us, whereby we are morally responsible for the existence of slavery, are horribly inhuman and wicked, and we cannot carry them out for the sake of their evil company.

By the dissolution of the Union we shall give the finishing blow to the slave system; and then God will make it possible for us to form a true, vital, enduring, all-embracing Union, from the Atlantic to the Pacific—one God to be worshipped, one Saviour to be revered, one policy to be carried out—freedom everywhere to all the people, without regard to complexion or race—and the blessing of God resting upon us all!

Jefferson Davis

Farewell to the Senate

U.S. Senate, Washington, D.C.
January 21, 1861

The death of John Calhoun left Mississippi Senator Jefferson Davis the primary advocate for the South. Davis supported the extension of slavery into the new states and territories and rejected northern interference on the issue of slavery, believing that slaves were better off under their masters and that slavery was not morally wrong. He had long held that the states had the legal right to secede from the Union, though he disagreed with Calhoun's doctrine of nullification. With the news of Mississippi's secession, Davis delivered his farewell speech to the Senate and shortly afterward became president of the Confederacy.

I rise, Mr. President, for the purpose of announcing to the Senate that I have satisfactory evidence that the State of Mississippi, by a solemn ordinance of her people in convention assembled, has declared her separation from the United States. Under these circumstances, of course my functions are terminated here. It has seemed to me proper, however, that I should appear in the Senate to announce that fact to my associates, and I will say but very little more. . . .

It is known to Senators who have served with me here that I have for many years advocated, as an essential attribute of state sovereignty, the right of a state to secede from the Union. Therefore, if I had not believed there was justifiable cause; if I had thought that Mississippi was acting without sufficient provocation, or without an existing necessity, I should still, under my theory of the government, because of my allegiance to the state of which I am a citizen, have been bound by her action. I, however, may be permitted to say that I do think that she has justifiable cause, and I approve of her act. I

conferred with her people before that act was taken, counseled them then that, if the state of things which they appre-
hended should exist when the convention met, they should
take the action which they have now adopted.

I hope none who hear me will confound this expression of
mine with the advocacy of the right of a state to remain in the
Union, and to disregard its constitutional obligations by the
nullification of the law. Such is not my theory. Nullification
and secession, so often confounded, are indeed antagonistic
principles. . . .

This is done not in hostility to others, not to injure any section of the country, not even for our own pecuniary benefit;
but from the high and solemn motive of defending and protecting the rights we inherited, and which it is our sacred duty
to transmit unshorn to our children.

I find in myself, perhaps, a type of the general feeling of my
constituents toward yours. I am sure I feel no hostility to you,
Senators from the North. I am sure there is not one of you,
whatever sharp discussion there may have been between us, to
whom I cannot now say, in the presence of my God, I wish
you well; and such, I am sure, is the feeling of the people
whom I represent toward those whom you represent. I therefore feel that I but express their desire when I say I hope, and
they hope, for peaceful relations with you, though we must
part. They may be mutually beneficial to us in the future, as
they have been in the past, if you so will it. The reverse may
bring disaster on every portion of the country; and if you will
have it thus, we will invoke the God of our fathers, who delivered them from the power of the lion, to protect us from the
ravages of the bear; and thus, putting our trust in God, and in
our own firm hearts and strong arms, we will vindicate the
right as best we may. . . .

Mr. President and Senators, having made the announcement which the occasion seemed to me to require, it only
remains for me to bid you a final adieu.

Abraham Lincoln

The Gettysburg Address

Gettysburg, Pennsylvania
November 19, 1863

By the time Abraham Lincoln took office as president in March 1861, seven states had seceded from the Union. Two years into the war, Union and Confederate forces met at the July 1863 Battle of Gettysburg, where 50,000 men were killed or wounded. At the November dedication of the battlefield cemetery there, Lincoln was not the featured speaker. A popular clergyman famous at that time for his oratory spoke for over two hours before the president's turn came to make his few remarks. Now that other speaker is largely forgotten, and Lincoln's short tribute to those who died and to the future of the Union is known as one of the greatest in our language.

☆ ☆

Four score and seven years ago our fathers brought forth on this continent, a new nation, conceived in liberty, and dedicated to the proposition that all men are created equal.

Now we are engaged in a great civil war, testing whether that nation or any nation so conceived and so dedicated, can long endure. We are met on a great battle-field of that war. We have come to dedicate a portion of that field, as a final resting place for those who here gave their lives that that nation might live. It is altogether fitting and proper that we should do this.

But, in a larger sense, we can not dedicate—we can not consecrate—we can not hallow—this ground. The brave men, living and dead, who struggled here, have consecrated it, far above our poor power to add or detract. The world will little note, nor long remember what we say here, but it can never forget what they did here. It is for us the living, rather, to be dedicated here to the unfinished work which they who fought here have thus far so nobly advanced. It is rather for us to be here dedicated to the great task remaining before us—that from these honored dead we take increased devotion to that cause for which they gave the last full measure of devotion—that we here highly resolve that these dead shall not have died in vain—that this nation, under God, shall have a new birth of freedom—and that government of the people, by the people, for the people, shall not perish from the earth.

Abraham Lincoln

"With Malice toward None, with Charity for All"

Washington, D.C.
March 4, 1865

With Civil War victories going increasingly to the Union and the war's close in sight, Abraham Lincoln was elected president for a second term. His brilliant second inaugural address spoke of the need to end the war and to heal the nation. Just a month later, he was killed by an assassin.

☆ ☆

Fellow countrymen: At this second appearing to take the oath of the presidential office, there is less occasion for an extended address than there was at first. . . .

On the occasion corresponding to this four years ago, all thoughts were anxiously directed to an impending civil war. All dreaded it, all sought to avoid it. While the inaugural address was being delivered from this place, devoted altogether to saving the Union without war, insurgent agents were in the city seeking to destroy it with war—seeking to dissolve the Union and divide the effects by negotiation. Both parties deprecated war, but one of them would make war rather than let the nation survive, and the other would accept war rather than let it perish, and the war came.

One-eighth of the whole population were colored slaves, not distributed generally over the Union, but localized in the Southern part of it. These slaves constituted a peculiar and powerful interest. All knew that this interest was somehow the cause of the war. To strengthen, perpetuate, and extend this interest was the object for which the insurgents would rend the Union by war, while the government claimed no right to do more than to restrict the territorial enlargement of it.

Neither party expected for the war the magnitude or the

duration which it has already attained. . . . Both read the same
Bible and pray to the same God, and each invokes His aid
against the other. It may seem strange that any men should
dare to ask a just God's assistance in wringing their bread
from the sweat of other men's faces, but let us judge not that
we be not judged. The prayer of both could not be answered.
That of neither has been answered fully. The Almighty has
His own purposes. . . .

Fondly do we hope, fervently do we pray, that this mighty
scourge of war may speedily pass away. Yet if God wills that it
continue until all the wealth piled by the bondsman's two
hundred and fifty years of unrequited toil shall be sunk, and
until every drop of blood drawn with the lash shall be paid by
another drawn with the sword, as was said three thousand
years ago, so still it must be said, that "the judgments of the
Lord are true and righteous altogether."

With malice toward none, with charity for all, with firm-
ness in the right as God gives us to see the right, let us finish
the work we are in, to bind up the nation's wounds, to care for
him who shall have borne the battle, and for his widow and
for his orphan, to do all which may achieve and cherish a just
and a lasting peace among ourselves and with all nations.

Henry M. Turner

"I Hold That I Am a Member of This Body"

Atlanta, Georgia
September 3, 1868

The Reconstruction-era Civil Rights Act of 1866 and the Fourteenth Amendment in 1868 established citizenship for African Americans for the first time, meaning they could vote and hold office. Henry McNeal Turner, a U.S. Army chaplain during the Civil War, was a delegate to the Georgia Constitutional Convention (Congress required Southern states to draw up new constitutions after the war). In 1868, Turner was elected to the Georgia House of Representatives from Bibb County. When he and 26 other black congressmen were expelled because of their race, he angrily addressed the Georgia House. Repeated protests to Washington resulted in their readmittance in 1869.

☆ ☆

Mr. Speaker: Before proceeding to argue this question upon its intrinsic merits, I wish the members of this House to understand the position that I take. I hold that I am a member of this body. Therefore, sir, I shall neither fawn or cringe before any party, nor stoop to beg them for my rights. Some of my colored fellow members, in the course of their remarks, took occasion to appeal to the sympathies of Members on the opposite side, and to eulogize their character for magnanimity. It reminds me very much, sir, of slaves begging under the lash. I am here to demand my rights, and to hurl thunderbolts at the men who would dare to cross the threshold of my manhood. There is an old aphorism which says, "Fight the Devil with fire," and if I should observe the rule in this instance, I wish gentlemen to understand that it is but fighting them with their own weapon. . . .

Whose Legislature is this? Is it a white man's Legislature, or is it a black man's Legislature? Who voted for a Constitutional

Convention, in obedience to the mandate of the Congress of the United States? Who first rallied around the standard of Reconstruction? Who set the ball of loyalty rolling in the State of Georgia? And whose voice was heard on the hills and in the valleys of this State? It was the voice of the brawny-armed Negro, with the few humanitarian-hearted white men who came to our assistance. . . . And there are persons in this Legislature to-day, who are ready to spit their poison in my face, while they themselves opposed, with all their power, the ratification of this Constitution. They question my right to a seat in this body, to represent the people whose legal votes elected me. This objection, sir, is an unheard of monopoly of power. . . .

Why, sir, though we are not white, we have accomplished much. We have pioneered civilization here; we have built up your country; we have worked in your fields, and garnered your harvests, for two hundred and fifty years! And what do we ask of you in return? Do we ask you for compensation for the sweat our fathers bore for you—for the tears you have caused, and the hearts you have broken, and the lives you have curtailed, and the blood you have spilled? Do we ask retaliation? We ask it not. We are willing to let the dead past bury its dead; but we ask you now for our RIGHTS. . . .

You may expel us, gentlemen, but I firmly believe that you will someday repent it. The black man cannot protect a country, if the country doesn't protect him; and if, tomorrow, a war should arise, I would not raise a musket to defend a country where my manhood is denied.

George Graham Vest

Eulogy on the Dog

Warrensburg, Missouri
September 23, 1870

In 1870, a Warrensburg, Missouri, sheep farmer was accused of shooting a prized hunting dog named Old Drum when the dog strayed onto his property. At his trial, a country lawyer named George Graham Vest gave a courtroom tribute that brought the jury to tears and won the case for the hound's owner, who received a judgment for $500, more than three times the maximum $150 allowed. Vest later served for 20 years as a senator from Missouri. A statue of Old Drum stands today in Warrensburg.

☆ ☆

Gentlemen of the jury:

The best friend a man has in the world may turn against him and become his enemy. His son or daughter that he has reared with loving care may prove ungrateful. Those who are nearest and dearest to us, those whom we trust with our happiness and our good name may become traitors to their faith. The money that a man has, he may lose. It flies away from him, perhaps when he needs it most. A man's reputation may be sacrificed in a moment of ill-considered action. The people who are prone to fall on their knees to do us honor when success is with us may be the first to throw the stone of malice when failure settles its cloud upon our heads.

The one absolutely unselfish friend that man can have in this selfish world, the one that never deserts him, the one that never proves ungrateful or treacherous is his dog. A man's dog stands by him in prosperity and in poverty, in health and in sickness. He will sleep on the cold ground, where the wintry winds blow and the snow drives fiercely, if only he may be near his master's side. He will kiss the hand that has no food to offer; he will lick the wounds and sores that come in encounter with the roughness of the world. He guards the sleep of his pauper master as if he were a prince. When all other friends desert, he remains. When riches take wings, and reputation falls to pieces, he is as constant in his love as the sun in its journey through the heavens.

If fortune drives the master forth an outcast in the world, friendless and homeless, the faithful dog asks no higher privilege than that of accompanying him, to guard him against danger, to fight against his enemies. And when the last scene of all comes, and death takes his master in its embrace and his body is laid away in the cold ground, no matter if all other friends pursue their way, there by the graveside will the noble dog be found, his head between his paws, his eyes sad, but open in alert watchfulness, faithful and true even in death.

Cochise, Chiricahua Apache Chief

"We Will Remain at Peace with Your People Forever"

Canada Alamosa, New Mexico
March 20-21, 1872

After the pointless killing of members of his family by an inexperienced U.S. Army officer and his troops, the Chiricahua Apache Chief Cochise warred with the United States for years. He was renowned for his courage and military ability and for the unhesitating obedience he drew from his followers. During negotiations for the removal of his band to a reservation in Arizona, he addressed General Gordon Granger at Canada Alamosa, New Mexico. The speech was recalled many years later by Henry Stuart Turrill, a member of Granger's staff that day, in his own 1909 address to a New York historical society.

☆ ☆

This for a very long time has been the home of my people. . . . We came to these mountains about us; no one lived here, and so we took them for our home and country. Here we grew from the first feeble band to be a great people and covered the whole country as the clouds cover the mountains. Many people came to our country. First the Spanish, with their horses and their iron shirts, their long knives and guns, great wonders to my simple people. We fought some, but they never tried to drive us from our homes in these mountains. After many years the Spanish soldiers were driven away and the Mexican ruled the land. With these, little wars came, but we were now a strong people, and we did not fear them.

At last in my youth came the white man, under your people. . . . I have fought long and as best I could against you. I have destroyed many of your people, but where I have destroyed one white man many have come in his place; where an Indian has been killed, there has been none to come in his place, so that the great people that welcomed you with acts of kindness to this land are now but a feeble band that fly before your soldiers as the deer before the hunter, and must all perish if this war continues.

I have come to you, not from any love for you or for your great father in Washington, or from any regard for his or your wishes, but as a conquered chief, to try to save alive the few people that still remain to me. I am the last of my family, a family that for very many years have been the leaders of this people; and on me depends their future, whether they shall utterly vanish from the land or that a small remnant remain for a few years to see the sun rise over these mountains, their home.

I here pledge my word, a word that has never been broken, that if your great father will set aside a part of my own country, where I and my little band can live, we will remain at peace with your people forever. . . . I have spoken.

Susan B. Anthony

"Are Women Persons?"

Rochester, New York
June 1873

Susan B. Anthony, the daughter of a Massachusetts Quaker abolitionist, labored unflaggingly as a leader of the movement for woman suffrage, or voting rights. Along with Elizabeth Cady Stanton, she formed the National Woman Suffrage Association in 1869. In the 1872 presidential election, Anthony was arrested and fined $100 for voting illegally in Rochester, New York. She refused to pay the fine. Although she was not allowed to speak in her own defense in court, she traveled the county defending her actions before numerous audiences in the month before her trial.

☆ ☆

Friends and fellow citizens, I stand before you tonight under indictment for the alleged crime of having voted at the last presidential election, without having a lawful right to vote. It shall be my work this evening to prove to you that in thus voting, I not only committed no crime but, instead, simply exercised my citizen's rights, guaranteed to me and all United States citizens by the National Constitution, beyond the power of any state to deny. . . .

The preamble of the federal Constitution says:

"We, the people of the United States, in order to form a more perfect union, establish justice, insure domestic tranquillity, provide for the common defense, promote the general welfare, and secure the blessings of liberty to ourselves and our posterity, do ordain and establish this Constitution for the United States of America."

It was we, the people; not we, the white male citizens; nor yet we, the male citizens; but we, the whole people, who formed the Union. And we formed it, not to give the blessings of liberty, but to secure them; not to the half of ourselves and the half of our posterity, but to the whole people—women as well as men. And it is a downright mockery to talk to women of their enjoyment of the blessings of liberty while they are denied the use of the only means of securing them provided by this democratic-republican government—the ballot. . . .

For any state to make sex a qualification that must ever result in the disfranchisement of one entire half of the people is to pass a bill of attainder, or an ex post facto law, and is therefore a violation of the supreme law of the land. By it the blessings of liberty are forever withheld from women and their female posterity. To them this government has no just powers derived from the consent of the governed. To them this government is not a democracy. It is not a republic. It is an odious aristocracy; a hateful oligarchy of sex; the most hateful aristocracy ever established on the face of the globe; . . . which makes father, brothers, husband, sons, the oligarchs over the mother and sisters, the wife and daughters, of every household—which ordains all men sovereigns, all women subjects, carries dissension, discord, and rebellion into every home of the nation. . . .

Webster, Worcester, and Bouvier all define a citizen to be a person in the United States, entitled to vote and hold office.

The only question left to be settled now is: Are women persons? And I hardly believe any of our opponents will have the hardihood to say they are not. Being persons, then, women are citizens; and no state has a right to make any law, or to enforce any old law, that shall abridge their privileges or immunities. Hence, every discrimination against women in the constitutions and laws of the several states is today null and void, precisely as is every one against Negroes. . . .

We no longer petition Legislature or Congress to give us the right to vote. We appeal to the women everywhere to exercise their too long neglected "citizen's right to vote." We appeal to the inspectors of election everywhere to receive the votes of all United States citizens as it is their duty to do. . . .

And it is on this line that we propose to fight our battle for the ballot—all peaceably, but nevertheless persistently through to complete triumph, when all United States citizens shall be recognized as equals before the law.

Chief Joseph and his family.

Chief Joseph, Nez Perce

"I Will Fight No More Forever"

Snake Creek, Montana
October 5, 1877

Protesting the fraudulent sale of their land, Chief Joseph and his Nez Perce tribe refused to give up their territory in Oregon. Threatened with forcible removal, they tried to escape to Canada while desperately fighting off the U.S. Army in a war noted for brilliant military maneuvers by the tribe. After traveling more than 1,000 miles over rugged terrain, the outnumbered Nez Perce were captured only thirty miles from Canada. In bitterly cold weather with five inches of snow on the ground, Chief Joseph made this poignant address at his surrender to Generals O. Howard and Nelson Miles, as recorded by Lieutenant Wood of Howard's staff.

☆ ☆

Tell General Howard I know his heart. What he told me before, I have it in my heart. I am tired of fighting. Our chiefs are killed; Looking Glass is dead, Ta-Hool-Hool-Shute is dead. The old men are all dead. It is the young men who say "Yes" or "No." He who led on the young men is dead. It is cold, and we have no blankets; the little children are freezing to death. My people, some of them, have run away to the hills, and have no blankets, no food. No one knows where they are—perhaps freezing to death. I want to have time to look for my children, and see how many of them I can find. Maybe I shall find them among the dead. Hear me, my chiefs! I am tired; my heart is sick and sad. From where the sun now stands I will fight no more forever.

☆
Elizabeth Cady Stanton
"The Solitude of Self"
U.S. Senate, Washington, D.C.
January 18, 1892

Elizabeth Cady Stanton was one of the first women to insist on the right to vote, and with other reformers in 1848 she held the first Woman's Rights Convention at Seneca Falls, New York, to discuss the position of woman in society. With Susan B. Anthony, she drafted the Seneca Falls Declaration of Sentiments, which proclaimed woman's equality with man and her freedom to address an audience, to vote, and to enter any profession. Still a brilliant orator at the age of 77, Stanton delivered her masterpiece, "The Solitude of Self," before the Senate Committee on Woman Suffrage.

☆ ☆

We ask for woman a voice in the government under which she lives; in the religion she is asked to believe; equality in social life, where she is the chief factor; a place in the trades and professions, where she may earn her bread, . . . because of her birthright to self-sovereignty; because, as an individual, she must rely on herself. . . .

To appreciate the importance of fitting every human soul for independent action, think for a moment of the immeasurable solitude of self. We come into the world alone, unlike all who have gone before us; we leave it alone, under circumstances peculiar to ourselves. No mortal ever has been, no mortal ever will be like the soul just launched on the sea of life. . . .

We ask for the complete development of every individual, first, for his own benefit and happiness. . . . Again, we ask complete individual development for the general good . . . of national life; and here each man must bear his share of the general burden. It is sad to see how soon friendless children

106

are left to bear their own burdens, before they can analyze their feelings; before they can even tell their joys and sorrows, they are thrown on their own resources. The great lesson that nature seems to teach us at all ages is self-dependence, self-protection, self-support.

What a touching instance of a child's solitude, of that hunger of the heart for love and recognition, in the case of the little girl who helped to dress a Christmas tree for the children of the family in which she served. On finding there was no present for herself, she slipped away in the darkness and spent the night in an open field sitting on a stone, and when found in the morning was weeping as if her heart would break. No mortal will ever know the thoughts that passed through the mind of that friendless child in the long hours of that cold night, with only the silent stars to keep her company. The mention of her case in the daily papers moved many generous hearts to send her presents, but in the hours of her keenest suffering she was thrown wholly on herself for consolation.

In youth our most bitter disappointments, our brightest hopes and ambitions, are known only to ourselves. Even our friendship and love we never fully share with another; there is something of every passion, in every situation, we conceal. Even so in our triumphs and our defeats. The successful candidate for the presidency, and his opponent, each has a solitude peculiarly his own, and good form forbids either to speak of his pleasure or regret. The solitude of the king on his throne and the prisoner in his cell differs in character and degree, but it is solitude, nevertheless.

We ask no sympathy from others in the anxiety and agony of a broken friendship or shattered love. When death sunders our nearest ties, alone we sit in the shadow of our affliction. . . . Seeing, then, that life must ever be a march and a battle, that each soldier must be equipped for his own protection, it is the height of cruelty to rob the individual of a single natural right.

To throw obstacles in the way of a complete education is like putting out the eyes; to deny the rights of property, like cutting off the hands. To deny political equality is to rob the ostracised of all self-respect; of credit in the market place; of recompense in the world of work; of a voice in those who make and administer the law; a choice in the jury before whom they are tried, and in the judge who decides their punishment. . . .

When suddenly roused at midnight, with the startling cry of "Fire! Fire!" to find the house over their heads in flames, do women wait for men to point the way to safety? . . .

Is it not the height of presumption in man to propose to represent her at the ballot box and the throne of grace, to do her voting in the State, her praying in the church, and to assume the position of High Priest at the family altar? . . . The talk of sheltering woman from the fierce storms of life is the sheerest mockery, for they beat on her from every point of the compass, just as they do on man, and with more fatal results, for he has been trained to protect himself, to resist, and to conquer.

There is a solitude which each and every one of us has always carried with him, more inaccessible than the ice-cold mountains, more profound than the midnight sea; the solitude of self. Our inner being which we call ourself, no eye nor touch of man or angel has ever pierced. . . .

Such is individual life. Who, I ask you, can take, dare take on himself the rights, the duties, the responsibilities of another human soul?

William Jennings Bryan stretches out his arms to mimic crucifixion upon the "cross of gold."

William Jennings Bryan

"A Cross of Gold"

Chicago, Illinois
July 9, 1896

Congressman William Jennings Bryan, Nebraska's "Great Commoner," devoted his political life to helping plain people in small towns against the interests of large cities and big business. Observing the worsening poverty of farmers and laborers, Bryan concluded that a shift in monetary policy from the gold standard to free silver would benefit the country. His memorable speech at the Democratic Convention won him the nomination for president in 1896, though he was barely a contender before he spoke. As he uttered the resounding last lines, Bryan held up his hands to mimic setting a crown upon his head, then stretched out his arms as though upon a cross.

☆ ☆

I come to speak to you in defense of a cause as holy as the cause of liberty—the cause of humanity. . . .

When you come before us and tell us that we are about to disturb your business interests, we reply that you have disturbed our business interests by your course.

We say to you that you have made the definition of a business man too limited in its application. The man who is employed for wages is as much a business man as his employer; . . . the farmer who goes forth in the morning and toils all day, who begins in spring and toils all summer, and who by the application of brain and muscle to the natural resources of the country creates wealth is as much a business man as the man who goes upon the board of trade and bets upon the price of grain; the miners who go down a thousand feet into the earth. . . are as much business men as the few financial magnates who, in a back room, corner the money of the world. We come to speak of this broader class of business men.

Ah, my friends, we say not one word against those who live upon the Atlantic Coast, but the hardy pioneers who have braved all the dangers of the wilderness, who have made the desert to blossom as the rose— . . . these people, we say, are as deserving of the consideration of our party as any people in this country. It is for these that we speak. We do not come as aggressors. Our war is not a war of conquest; we are fighting in the defense of our homes, our families, and posterity. We have petitioned, and our petitions have been scorned; we have entreated, and our entreaties have been disregarded; we have begged, and they have mocked when our calamity came. We beg no longer; we entreat no more; we petition no more. We defy them! . . .

We go forth confident that we shall win. Why? Because upon the paramount issue of this campaign there is not a spot of ground upon which the enemy will dare to challenge battle. If they tell us that the gold standard is a good thing, we shall point to their platform and tell them that their platform pledges the party to get rid of the gold standard and substitute bimetallism. If the gold standard is a good thing, why try to get rid of it? . . .

If they tell us that the gold standard is the standard of civilization, we reply to them that this, the most enlightened of all the nations of the earth has never declared for a gold standard and that both the great parties this year are declaring against it. If the gold standard is the standard of civilization, why, my friends, should we not have it? . . .

You come to us and tell us that the great cities are in favor of the gold standard; we reply that the great cities rest upon our broad and fertile prairies. Burn down your cities and leave our farms, and your cities will spring up again as if by magic; but destroy our farms, and the grass will grow in the streets of every city in the country.

My friends, we declare that this nation is able to legislate for its own people on every question, without waiting for the aid or consent of any other nation on earth; and upon that issue we expect to carry every state in the Union. . . . Having behind us the producing masses of this nation and the world, supported by the commercial interests, the laboring interests, and the toilers everywhere, we will answer their demand for a gold standard by saying to them, You shall not press down upon the brow of labor this crown of thorns; you shall not crucify mankind upon a cross of gold.

☆

Russell Conwell

"Acres of Diamonds"

Philadelphia, Pennsylvania
Late 1890s

Before the invention of radio and television, a popular pastime was attending inspirational and humorous lectures given by touring speakers. Like Ralph Waldo Emerson and Mark Twain, Russell Conwell became one of the most successful lecturers in the country. He fought for the North in the Civil War, joined the Baptist ministry, and founded Temple University in Philadelphia. A youthful war memory closes his "Acres of Diamonds" speech, the jewel in his repertoire, given innumerable times over fifty years on the lecture circuit in every state of the Union.

☆ ☆

Suppose I were to go through this house and shake hands with each of you and say: "Please introduce me to the great men and women in this hall tonight."

You would say: "Great men! We don't have any here. There are none in this audience. If you want to find great men you must go to some other part of the world! Great men always come from somewhere else." . . .

But there are just as great men hearing me speak tonight as there are elsewhere, and yet, who, because of their simplicity, are not now appreciated. . . .

We teach our young people to believe that all the great people are away off. I heard a professor in an Illinois college say that "nearly all the great men are dead." We don't want him in Philadelphia.

The greatest men are living now, and will only be exceeded by the generations to come; and he who appreciates that fact will look around him and will respect his neighbor, and will respect his environment. I have to say tonight that the great men of the world are those who appreciate that which is next to them. . . .

Some young man is saying: "There is going to be a great man here, although I don't know of any now."

"Young man when are you going to be great?"

"When I am elected to some political office, then I will be great."

Oh young man, learn right now, . . . greatness is intrinsic, it is in the personality, not in the office. If you are not great as an individual before you go into the office, you may rattle around in it after you get in, like "shot in a tin pan." There will be no greatness there. You will hold the office for a year or more and never be heard of again. There are greater things than political office. Many a young man's fortune has been made by being defeated when he was up for political office. You never saw a really great man in office who did not take the office at a sacrifice to himself.

Another young man says: "There is going to be a great man here."

"When?"

"When there comes a war!" . . .

Young man, remember greatness does not consist in holding office, even in war. The office does not make the great man. . . .

I will give one more illustration. I don't like to give it. I don't know how I ever fell into the habit. Indeed, it was first given off-hand to a Grand Army post of which I was a member. I hesitate to give it now.

I close my eyes and I can see my own native hills once more. . . . I can see the crowd again that was there in that wartime, 1864, dressed in red, white and blue; the flags flying, the band playing. I see a platoon of soldiers who have returned from one term of service and reenlisted for the second, and are now to be received by the mountain town. Oh, well do I remember the day. I was captain of the company. Although in my teens, I was marching at the head of that company and puffed out with pride. A cambric needle would have burst me all to pieces! I am sincerely ashamed of the whole thing now. But what august pride, then in my youth, marching at the head of my troops, being received by the country town authorities!

We marched into the Town Hall. They seated my soldiers in the middle of the hall, and the crowds came in on the right and on the left. . . . The good old mayor of the town . . . saw me on the front seat, and he came right forward and invited me up on the platform with the "Selectmen." Invited me, me! up on the stand with the town officers! Why, no town officer ever took any notice of me before I went to war; yet perhaps I ought not to say that, because one of them, I remember, did advise a teacher to "whale" me. . . .

The mayor waited for quite a while, and then came forward to the table. Oh, that speech! . . . He had never delivered an address before. He thought the office would make him an orator. But he forgot that a man must speak his piece as a boy if he wishes to become an orator as a man. . . .

"Fellow citizens!"—and then he paused until his fingers and knees shook, and began to swallow, then turned aside to look at his manuscript.

"Fellow citizens: We are—we are—we are—we are very happy. . . . We are especially,—we are especially pleased to see with us tonight this young hero,—(that meant me, friends, remember he said that; if he hadn't said that I wouldn't have been egotistic enough to refer to it today, I assure you)—who, in imagination,—we have seen leading his troops on to the deadly breach. We have seen his shining—we have seen his shining—his shining sword—we have seen his shining sword, flashing in the sunlight, as he shouted to his troops, 'Come on!'"

Oh, dear, dear, dear! He was a good old man, but how little he knew about the War. If he had known anything about war at all, he ought to have known that it is next to a crime for an officer of infantry ever, in time of danger, to go ahead of his men. I, with "my shining sword flashing in the sunlight," and calling to my troops, "Come on!" I never did it. Do you suppose I would go in front of my men to be shot in front by the enemy, and in the back by my own men? It is no place for an officer. The place for an officer in time of danger is behind the private soldier, . . . for if your officers and your generals were killed on the first discharge, where would the plan of the battle be?

How ashamed I was of the whole affair [in the Town Hall that day]. . . . Some of those men had carried that boy, [me], across the Carolina rivers. Some of them had given him their last draught of coffee. One of them had leaped in front of him and had his cheek bone shot away; he had leaped in front of the boy to save his life. Some were not there at all, and the tears flowing from the eyes of the widows and orphans showed that they had gone down for their country. Yet in the good man's speech he scarcely noticed those who had died; the hero of the hour was that boy, [me]. We do not know even now where many of those comrades do sleep. They went down to death. . . . But I do know this, they were brave men. I know they went down before a brave foe, fighting for a cause both believed to be right. Yet the hero of this hour was this boy. He was an officer, and they were only private soldiers.

I learned a lesson then I will never forget, until the bell of time ceases to swing for me,—that greatness consists not in holding an office. Greatness really consists in doing great deeds with little means,—in the accomplishment of vast purposes; from the private ranks of life—in benefiting one's own neighborhood, in blessing one's own city, the community in which he dwells. There, and there only, is the great test of human goodness and human ability. He who waits for an office before he does great and noble deeds must fail altogether.

☆

Harry Gladstone

To the Machine Tenders Union

New York City
August 13, 1898

Many children in the early 1900s had to work to help their families survive. Working conditions were harsh, and few laws protected laborers. Adult workers organized unions to pressure employers to provide better conditions. Harry Gladstone was a 15-year-old immigrant boy who attended school for only three years before he began working as a machine tender or "basting puller." When he organized a union of 75 working children, some only 12 years old, he became known as the "boy agitator of the East Side." Harry gave a reporter and a crowd of children an example of the speech he planned to give that afternoon to his Machine Tenders Union.

☆ ☆

Fellow workmen, I tell you to stick together.

Think about your poor fathers and mothers you have got to support. [Think] of the schools and how you can't go there to get your education, but must spend from 14 to 15 hours a day in a pest-hole, pulling bastings, turning collars and sleeves, and running around as if you were crazy.

If you don't look out for yourselves, who will? You have not had time to grow up, to get strength for work, when you must spend your dearest days in the sweatshop. Think of the way your mothers kiss you, how they love you, and how they shed tears over you, because they see their dear boys treated like slaves.

Try to make a few dollars for them at least. Then you will come home and kiss your mamas and say "Don't cry, dear Mama. Here, I've brought you some money for rent, or for a Sabbath meal."

The only way to get the bosses to pay us good wages is to stick together, so let us be true to our union.

Mother Jones assists a miner's child in putting on her shoe.

Mother Jones

To the United Mine Workers of America

Indianapolis, Indiana
January 25, 1901

At the turn of the last century, coal miners toiled in horrendous conditions, facing death daily from cave-ins and disease from breathing coal dust. Children were injured in the "breakers," where machines broke the coal and "breaker boys" picked out the rocks. In this setting, Mary Harris Jones labored tirelessly into her nineties agitating on behalf of poorly paid and mistreated workers. This heroic and fearless woman, taking up her chosen work after the deaths (from yellow fever) of her husband and children, and jailed repeatedly for leading labor strikes, became "Mother" Jones to the coal miners. Here she addresses the convention of the United Mine Workers of America on the exploitation of working children.

☆☆

117

Fellow toilers, you have done your work magnificently and well; but we have before us yet the grandest and greatest work of civilization. We have before us the emancipation of the children of this nation. . . .

Now when the father comes home the first question he asks is "Mary, is it a boy or a girl?" When she answers, "It is a boy, John," he says, "Well, thank God! He will soon be able to go to the breakers and help earn a living with me." If it is a girl there is no loving kiss, no caress for her for she cannot be put to the breakers to satisfy capitalistic greed. But my friends, the capitalistic class has met you face to face today to take the girls as well as the boys out of the cradle. Wherever you are in mighty numbers they have brought their factories to take your daughters and slaughter them on the altar of capitalistic greed. They have built their mines and breakers to take your boys out of the cradle; they have built their factories to take your girls; they have built on the bleeding, quivering hearts of yourselves and your children their palaces. They have built their magnificent yachts and palaces; they have brought the sea from mid-ocean up to their homes where they can take their baths—and they don't give you a chance to go to the muddy Missouri and take a bath in it.

My friends, we are here to tell you that the mothers of this nation will join hands with you in the mighty conflict ahead. We are here to tell you that no more will the mother reach down into the cradle and take the babe out of it and sell it for so many hours a day to their capitalistic masters.

I stand here today to appeal to you in behalf of the helpless children. I want all of you to go to your homes and act as missionaries in their behalf. Get your brothers into your organization, bring them up under the banner of a coming civilization where we can take the little children and put them in the school room and educate them for the benefit of the nation.

One stormy night at Coleraine I went down to see the little breaker boys as they came into the schoolroom. The little fellows came to me and said they wanted to get organized, because they had a mighty mean boss and they wanted to lick him. I explained to them that they are in bondage owing to the indifference of their own fathers and mothers. I told them that there was a glimmer of light for them, and that I hoped their condition would soon be better. Then I said to them, "In all the years your father has worked what has he now as a compensation for his years and years of labor?" One little fellow, whose face was old and withered with the hard tasks he had to perform, stood up and looked me in the face and said, "Mother Jones, all my father has is the hump on his back and the miner's asthma." It occurred to me that that child was a far better philosopher than the father was. . . .

When the children stood on the platform of a hall we had hired for them to expose the corporations one little boy of twelve came to the front and told us that he worked thirteen hours at night, that they paid him one cent an hour. . . .

We should clasp our hands and come out together in defense of these little children. I can see an appeal in their eyes which seems to ask what they have done that they should be battered and knocked about as they are. There are children under age in those factories. . . . While the factory inspector is being taken over the mill there are children hidden in closets and locked up there until he leaves. These things are all wrong. . . .

I want to say to you that the man or woman who would undertake to sell and rob and plunder those children is not fit to be classed with human beings. The man or woman who would witness such scenes as I have witnessed in West Virginia would betray God Almighty if he betrayed those people. Ah, my brothers, I shall consider it an honor if, when you write my epitaph upon my tombstone, you say, "Died fighting their battles in West Virginia."

Florence Kelley

"Freeing the Children from Toil"

Portland, Oregon
June 28, 1905

The social worker and reformer Florence Kelley made it her life's work to bring an end to child labor. In 1902, she founded the National Child Labor Committee, which sent the photographer Lewis Hine to document the conditions of working children. At the 1905 convention of the National American Woman Suffrage Association, she spoke on the hope for ending the exploitation of children in the nation's factories once women had the vote. Most states enacted child labor laws when women received the right to vote in 1920, but it wasn't until 1938 that the Fair Labor Standards Act established a national minimum working age to protect children.

To-night while we sleep, several thousand little girls will be working in textile mills, all the night through, in the deafening noise of the spindles and looms spinning and weaving cotton and woolen, silks and ribbons for us to buy. . . . If the mothers and the teachers in Georgia could vote, would the Georgia Legislature have refused at every session for the last three years to stop the work in the mills of children under twelve years of age?

Would the New Jersey Legislature have passed that shameful repeal bill enabling girls fourteen years to work all night, if the mothers in New Jersey were enfranchised? Until the mothers in the great industrial States are enfranchised, we shall none of us be able to free our consciences from participation in this great evil. No one in this room to-night can feel free from such participation. The children make our shoes in the shoe factories; they knit our stockings, our knitted underwear in the knitting factories. They spin and weave our cotton underwear in the cotton mills. Children braid straw for our hats, they spin and weave the silk and velvet wherewith we trim our hats. They stamp buckles and metal ornaments of all kinds, as well as pins and hat-pins. Under the sweating system, tiny children make artificial flowers and neckwear for us to buy. They carry bundles of garments from the factories to the tenements, little beasts of burden, robbed of school life that they may work for us.

We do not wish this. We prefer to have our work done by men and women. But we are almost powerless. Not wholly powerless, however, are citizens who enjoy the right of petition. For myself, I shall use this power in every possible way until the right to the ballot is granted, and then I shall continue to use both.

What can we do to free our consciences? There is one line of action by which we can do much. We can enlist the workingmen on behalf of our enfranchisement just in proportion as we strive with them to free the children. No labor organization in this country ever fails to respond to an appeal for help in the freeing of the children.

For the sake of the children, for the Republic in which these children will vote after we are dead, and for the sake of our cause, we should enlist the workingmen voters, with us, in this task of freeing the children from toil.

☆

Mark Twain

"In Behalf of Simplified Spelling"

New York City
September 19, 1906

Mark Twain, whose real name was Samuel Clemens, created many of America's favorite fictional characters, notably Huckleberry Finn and Tom Sawyer. Known as a teller of comic tall tales, Twain was a popular guest speaker at social gatherings. At the annual Associated Press banquet in New York in 1906, he amused the audience of journalists with his speech promoting the movement for simplified spelling, a reform begun by Andrew Carnegie but opposed by the clergy and the British, among others.

☆ ☆

I am here to make an appeal to the nations in behalf of the simplified spelling. I have come here because they cannot all be reached except through you. There are only two forces that can carry light to all the corners of the globe—only two—the sun in the heavens and the Associated Press down here. I may seem to be flattering the sun, but I do not mean it so; I am meaning only to be just and fair all around. You speak with a million voices; no one can reach so many races, so many hearts and intellects, as you. . . .

And so I beg you, I beseech you—oh, I implore you to spell . . . in our simplified forms. Do this daily, constantly, persistently, for three months—only three months—it is all I ask. The infallible result?—victory, victory, all down the line. . . . And we shall be rid of phthisis and phthisic and pneumonia, and pneumatics, and diphtheria and pterodactyl, and all those other insane words.

Do I seem to be seeking the good of the world? That is the idea. It is my public attitude; privately I am merely seeking my own profit. . . . In 1883, when the simplified spelling movement first tried to make a noise, I was indifferent to it; more—I even irreverently scoffed at it. What I needed was an object lesson, you see. It is the only way to teach some people. Very well, I got it. At that time I was scrambling along, earning the family's bread on magazine work at seven cents a word, compound words at single rates, just as it is in the dark present. I was the property of a magazine, a seven-cent slave under a boiler iron contract.

One day there came a note from the editor requiring me to write ten pages on this revolting text: "Considerations concerning the alleged subterranean holophotal extemporaneousness of the conchyliaceous superimbrication of the ornithorhyncus, as foreshadowed by the unintelligibility of its plesiosaurian anisodactylous aspects."

Ten pages of that. Each and every word a seventeen-jointed vestibuled railroad train. Seven cents a word. I saw starvation staring the family in the face. . . .

I said, "You want ten pages of those rumbling, great long summer thunder peals, and you expect to get them at seven cents a word?"

He said, "A word's a word, and seven cents is the contract; what are you going to do about it?"

I said, "Jackson, this is cold-blooded oppression. What's an average English word?"

He said, "Six letters."

I said, "Nothing of the kind; that's French, and includes the spaces between the words; an average English word is four letters and a half. By hard honest labor I've dug all the large words out of my vocabulary and shaved it down until the average is three letters and a half. I can put 1,200 words on your page, and there's not another man alive that can come within two hundred of it. . . . So I never write 'metropolis' for seven cents, because I can get the same money for 'city.' I never write 'policeman,' because I can get the same price for 'cop'. And so on and so on. I never write 'valetudinarian' at all, for not even hunger and wretchedness can humble me to the point where I will do a word like that for seven cents; I wouldn't do it for fifteen. Examine your shameful text, please; count the words."

He counted and said it was 24. I asked him to count the letters. He made it 203.

I said, "Now, I hope you will see the whole size of your contemplated crime. With my vocabulary I would make 60 words out of those 203 letters and get $4.20 for it; whereas for your inhuman 24 I would get only $1.68. . . . I do not wish to work upon this scandalous job by the piece. I want to be hired by the year." He coldly refused.

I said, "Then for the sake of the family, if you have no feeling for me, you ought at least to allow me overtime on that word 'extemporaneousness.'" Again he coldly refused. I seldom say a harsh word to anyone, but I was not master of myself then, and I spoke right out and called him an anisodactylous plesiosaurian conchyliaceous ornithorhyncus, and rotten to the heart with holophotal subterranean extemporaneousness. God forgive me for that wanton crime; he lived only two hours!

From that day to this I have been a devoted and hard-working member of that heaven-born institution, the International Association for the Prevention of Cruelty to Authors, and now I am laboring with Carnegie's Simplified Committee, and with my heart in the work.

☆

Theodore Roosevelt

Citizenship in a Republic

Paris, France
April 23, 1910

Shy and delicate as a boy, Theodore Roosevelt overcame his limitations to become a man of vigor. He was nominated for vice president while governor of New York and honed his speaking ability by trying to match William Jennings Bryan's numberless campaign talks. The assassination of McKinley brought Roosevelt to the presidency, where his message was always one of strength, decency, and individual responsibility. His speech at the Sorbonne University on citizenship in a republic comes from his collection The Strenuous Life. *The last paragraph below was quoted by Richard Nixon in his address on resigning the presidency.*

☆ ☆

To-day I shall speak to you on the subject of individual citizenship, the one subject of vital importance to you, my hearers, and to me and my countrymen, because you and we are citizens of great democratic republics. . . . With you here, and with us in my own home, in the long run, success or failure will be conditioned upon the way in which the average man, the average woman, does his or her duty, first in the ordinary, every-day affairs of life, and next in those great occasional crises which call for the heroic virtues. . . . Therefore it behooves us to do our best to see that the standard of the average citizen is kept high; and the average cannot be kept high unless the standard of the leaders is very much higher.

It is well if a large proportion of the leaders in any republic, in any democracy, are, as a matter of course, drawn from the classes represented in this audience to-day; but only provided that those classes possess the gifts of sympathy with plain people and of devotion to great ideals. . . .

Let the man of learning, the man of lettered leisure, beware of that queer and cheap temptation to pose to himself and to others as the cynic, as the man who has outgrown emotions and beliefs, the man to whom good and evil are as one. The poorest way to face life is to face it with a sneer. There are many men who feel a kind of twisted pride in cynicism; there are many who confine themselves to criticism of the way others do what they themselves dare not even attempt. There is no more unhealthy being, no man less worthy of respect, than he who either really holds, or feigns to hold, an attitude of sneering disbelief toward all that is great and lofty, whether in achievement or in that noble effort which, even if it fails, comes second to achievement. . . .

It is not the critic who counts; not the man who points out how the strong man stumbles, or where the doer of deeds could have done them better. The credit belongs to the man who is actually in the arena, whose face is marred by dust and sweat and blood; who strives valiantly; who errs, and comes short again and again, because there is no effort without error and shortcoming; but who does actually strive to do the deeds; who knows the great enthusiasms, the great devotions; who spends himself in a worthy cause; who at the best knows in the end the triumph of high achievement, and who at the worst, if he fails, at least fails while daring greatly, so that his place shall never be with those cold and timid souls who know neither victory nor defeat.

Rose Schneiderman

On the Triangle Shirtwaist Company Fire

New York City
April 2, 1911

*A Polish-born immigrant to New York, Rose Schneiderman was forced by desper-
ate poverty to leave school at 13 and work as a seamstress. At 21, she organized
her first union chapter and began to lead strikes in the clothing industry for better
working conditions. In 1911, 146 garment workers were killed in the horrifying
Triangle Shirtwaist factory fire. Many of those who died were young girls who
jumped from the ninth-floor sweatshop to escape the flames because the manage-
ment had locked the doors and blocked the fire escape. Some were girls Schneiderman knew from a shirtwaist-makers' strike, and she addressed an angry speech to
a public assembly at the Metropolitan Opera House.*

I would be a traitor to these poor burned bodies if I came
here to talk good fellowship. We have tried you good people of the public and we have found you wanting. The old
Inquisition had its rack and its thumbscrews and its instruments of torture with iron teeth. We know what these things
are today; the iron teeth are our necessities, the thumbscrews
are the high-powered and swift machinery close to which we
must work, and the rack is here in the firetrap structures that
will destroy us the minute they catch on fire.

This is not the first time girls have been burned alive in the
city. Every week I must learn of the untimely death of one of
my sister workers. Every year thousands of us are maimed.
The life of men and women is so cheap and property is so
sacred. There are so many of us for one job it matters little if
146 of us are burned to death.

We have tried you citizens; we are trying you now, and you
have a couple of dollars for the sorrowing mothers, brothers

and sisters by way of a charity gift. But every time the workers come out in the only way they know to protest against conditions which are unbearable the strong hand of the law is allowed to press down heavily upon us.

Public officials have only words of warning to us—warning that we must be intensely peaceable, and they have the workhouse just back of all their warnings. The strong hand of the law beats us back, when we rise, into the conditions that make life unbearable.

I can't talk fellowship to you who are gathered here. Too much blood has been spilled. I know from my experience it is up to the working people to save themselves. The only way they can save themselves is by a strong working-class movement.

John Jay Chapman

The Coatesville Address

Coatesville, Pennsylvania
August 18, 1912

A New York writer and poet and descendent of abolitionists, John Jay Chapman
was horrified by newspaper reports of the 1911 burning alive of a black man
named Walker, in Coatesville, Pennsylvania. One year later he traveled to
Coatesville to hold a memorial service on the anniversary of the murder. He
encountered hostility and suspicion, but rented an empty storefront and advertised
the service. Chapman gave his address, reproaching indifference to the cruel legacy
of slavery, to an audience of only three persons: a friend, an elderly black woman
visiting the area, and a local man he suspected of being a spy sent by the community.

☆ ☆

We are met to commemorate the anniversary of one of the most dreadful crimes in history—not for the purpose of condemning it, but to repent of our share in it. We do not start any agitation with regard to that particular crime. I understand that an attempt to prosecute the chief criminals has been made, and has entirely failed; because the whole community, and in a sense our whole people, are really involved in the guilt. The failure of the prosecution in this case, in all such cases, is only a proof of the magnitude of the guilt, and of the awful fact that everyone shares in it.

I will tell you why I am here; I will tell you what happened to me. When I read in the newspapers of August 14, a year ago, about the burning alive of a human being, and of how a few desperate, fiend-minded men had been permitted to torture a man chained to an iron bedstead, burning alive, thrust back by pitchforks when he struggled out of it, while around about stood hundreds of well-dressed American citizens, both from the vicinity and from afar, coming on foot and in wagons, assembling on telephone call, as if by magic, silent, whether from terror or indifference, fascinated and impotent, hundreds of persons watching this awful sight and making no attempt to stay the wickedness, and no one man among them all who was inspired to risk his life in an attempt to stop it, no one man to name the name of Christ, of humanity, of government! As I read the newspaper accounts of the scene enacted here in Coatesville a year ago, I seemed to get a glimpse into the unconscious soul of this country. I saw a seldom revealed picture of the American heart and of the American nature. I seemed to be looking into the heart of the criminal—a cold thing, an awful thing.

I said to myself, "I shall forget this, we shall all forget it; but it will be there. What I have seen is not an illusion. It is the truth. I have seen death in the heart of this people." For to look at the agony of a fellow-being and remain aloof means death in the heart of the onlooker. . . .

I saw during one moment something beyond all argument in the depth of its significance. You might call it the paralysis of the nerves about the heart in a people habitually and unconsciously given over to selfish aims, an ignorant people who knew not what spectacle they were providing, or what part they were playing in a judgment-play which history was exhibiting on that day.

No theories about the race problem, no statistics, legislation, or mere educational endeavor, can quite meet the lack which that day revealed in the American people. For what we saw was death. The people stood like blighted things, like ghosts about Acheron, waiting for someone or something to determine their destiny for them.

Whatever life itself is, that thing must be replenished in us. The opposite of hate is love, the opposite of cold is heat; what we need is the love of God and reverence for human nature. For one moment I knew that I had seen our true need; and I was afraid that I should forget it and that I should go about framing arguments and agitations and starting schemes of education, when the need was deeper than education. And I became filled with one idea, that I must not forget what I had seen, and that I must do something to remember it. And I am here to-day chiefly that I may remember that vision. It seems fitting to come to this town where the crime occurred and hold a prayer-meeting, so that our hearts may be turned to God through whom mercy may flow into us.

Let me say one thing more about the whole matter. The subject we are dealing with is not local. The act, to be sure, took place at Coatesville and everyone looked to Coatesville to follow it up. Some months ago I asked a friend who lives not far from here something about this case, and about the expected prosecutions, and he replied to me: "It wasn't in my county," and that made me wonder whose county it was in. And it seemed to be in my county. I live on the Hudson River; but I knew that this great wickedness that happened in Coatesville is not the wickedness of Coatesville nor of to-day. It is the wickedness of all America and of three hundred years—the wickedness of the slave trade. All of us are tinctured by it. No special place, no special persons, are to blame. A nation cannot practice a course of inhuman crime for three hundred years and then suddenly throw off the effects of it. Less than fifty years ago domestic slavery was abolished among us; and in one way and another the marks of that vice are in our faces. . . .

On the day of the calamity, those people in the automobiles came by the hundred and watched the torture, and passers-by came in a great multitude and watched it—and did nothing. On the next morning the newspapers spread the news and spread the paralysis until the whole country seemed to be helplessly watching this awful murder, as awful as anything ever done on the earth. . . . Someone may say that you and I cannot repent because we did not do the act. But we are involved in it. We are still looking on. . . .

This whole matter has been an historic episode; but it is a part, not only of our national history, but of the personal history of each one of us. With the great disease, slavery, came the climax, the war, and after the climax gradually began the cure, and in the process of cure comes now the knowledge of what the evil was. I say that our need is new life, and that books and resolutions will not save us, but only such disposition in our hearts and souls as will enable the new life, love, force, hope, virtue, which surround us always, to enter into us. . . .

The occasion is not small; the occasion looks back on three centuries and embraces a hemisphere. Yet the occasion is small compared with the truth it leads us to. For this truth touches all ages and affects every soul in the world.

Stephen S. Wise

Tribute to Lincoln

Springfield, Illinois
February 12, 1914

In 1908, two days of assaults against blacks in Springfield, Illinois, spurred reform-minded Americans into action. People were shocked that lynchings could happen in the home town of Abraham Lincoln. The next year on Lincoln's 100th birthday, Rabbi Stephen S. Wise of New York, a prominent Jewish leader, was one of the signers of "The Call," which led to the formation of the National Association for the Advancement of Colored People (NAACP). Five years later, he delivered this tribute for Lincoln's birthday in Springfield, the city where Lincoln began his life in politics and where he is buried.

☆ ☆

We dwell in times of great perplexity and are beset by far-reaching problems of social, industrial, and political import. We shall not greatly err if upon every occasion we consult the genius of Abraham Lincoln. We shall not falter nor swerve from the path of national righteousness if we live by the moral genius of the great American commoner. . . .

Lincoln is become for us the test of human worth, and we honor men in the measure in which they approach the absolute standard of Abraham Lincoln. . . .

In his lifetime Lincoln was maligned and traduced, but detraction during a man's lifetime affords no test of his life's value nor offers any forecast of history's verdict. It would almost seem as if the glory of immortality were anticipated in the life of the great by detraction and denial whilst yet they lived. When a Lincoln-like man arises, let us recognize and fitly honor him. There could be no poorer way of honoring the memory of Lincoln than to assume, as we sometimes do, that the race of Lincolns has perished from the earth, and that we shall never look upon his like again.

One way to ensure the passing of the Lincolns is to assume that another Lincoln can nevermore arise. Would we find Lincoln today, we must not seek him in the guise of a rail-splitter, nor as a wielder of the backwoods-man's ax, but as a mighty smiter of wrong in high places and low. . . .

I have sometimes thought that the noblest tribute paid to the memory of Lincoln was the word of Phillips Brooks in Westminster Abbey when, pointing out that the test of the world to every nation was "Show us your man," he declared that America names Lincoln. But the first word spoken after the death of Lincoln is truest and best—the word of Secretary of War Stanton, standing by the side of that scene of peace— "Now he belongs to the ages."

It was verdict and prophecy alike, for Lincoln is not America's, he is the world's; he belongs not to our age, but to the ages; and yet, though he belongs to all time and to all peoples, he is our own, for he was an American.

Woodrow Wilson

"An Oath of Allegiance to a Great Ideal"

Philadelphia, Pennsylvania
May 10, 1915

Woodrow Wilson was for many years a college professor and president of Princeton University. In 1912, after serving for two years as the governor of New Jersey, he became president of the United States. During his years in office, a flood of immigrants arrived in America. Congress proposed the Burnett bill in 1915 to reduce their numbers by restricting immigration to those who could read and write. Wilson vetoed the measure, saying it would go against everything the United States stood for to refuse admission to those who had been denied an education. Later that year, he addressed a group of newly naturalized Americans at the ceremony at which they received their citizenship.

☆ ☆

It warms my heart that you should give me such a reception, but it is not of myself that I wish to think to-night, but of those who have just become citizens of the United States. This is the only country in the world which experiences this constant and repeated rebirth. Other countries depend upon the multiplication of their own native people. This country is constantly drinking strength out of new sources by the voluntary association with it of great bodies of strong men and forward-looking women. And so by the gift of the free will of independent people, it is constantly being renewed from generation to generation by the same process by which it was originally created. It is as if humanity had determined to see to it that this great nation, founded for the benefit of humanity, should not lack for the allegiance of the people of the world.

You have just taken an oath of allegiance to the United States. Of allegiance to whom? Of allegiance to no one, unless it be God. Certainly not of allegiance to those who temporarily represent this great Government. You have taken an oath of allegiance to a great ideal, to a great body of principles, to a great hope of the human race. You have said, "We are going to America," not only to earn a living, not only to seek the things which it was more difficult to obtain where you were born, but to help forward the great enterprises of the human spirit—to let man know that everywhere in the world there are men who will cross strange oceans and go where a speech is spoken which is alien to them, knowing that, whatever the speech, there is but one longing and utterance of the human heart, and that is for liberty and justice.

And while you bring all countries with you, you come with a purpose of leaving all other countries behind you—bringing what is best of their spirit, but not looking over your shoulders and seeking to perpetuate what you intended to leave in them. I certainly would not be one even to suggest that a man ceases to love the home of his birth and the nation of his origin—these things are very sacred and ought not to be put out of our hearts—but it is one thing to love the place where you were born and it is another thing to dedicate yourself to the place to which you go. You cannot dedicate yourself to America unless you become in every respect and with every purpose of your will thorough Americans. You cannot become thorough Americans if you think of yourselves in groups. America does not consist of groups. A man who thinks of himself as belonging to a particular national group in America, has not yet become an American, and the man who goes among you to trade upon your nationality is no worthy son to live under the Stars and Stripes. . . .

So, if you come into this great nation as you have come, voluntarily seeking something that we have to give, . . . we cannot exempt you from the strife and the heartbreaking burden of the struggle of the day—that is common to mankind everywhere. We cannot exempt you from the loads you must carry; we can only make them light by the spirit in which they are carried. That is the spirit of hope, it is the spirit of liberty, it is the spirit of justice.

☆

Anna Howard Shaw

The Fundamental Principle of a Republic

Ogdensburg, New York
June 21, 1915

Anna Howard Shaw of Michigan was one of the most brilliant and effective of the woman's suffrage orators. As president of the National American Woman Suffrage Association, she spoke tirelessly across New York State in 1915 advocating passage of the referendum to give the vote to New York women. World War I had begun the previous year, but the United States remained neutral until Germany on May 7, 1915, sank the ocean liner Lusitania *with 128 Americans aboard. It appeared that the United States might have to fight, and Shaw argued that giving the vote to women would be a move toward future peace.*

☆ ☆

When I came into your hall tonight, I thought of the last time I was in your city. Twenty-one years ago I came here with Susan B. Anthony, and we came for exactly the same purpose as that for which we are here tonight. Boys have been born since that time and have become voters, and the women are still trying to persuade American men to believe in the fundamental principles of democracy, . . . that a government which claims to be a Republic should be a Republic, and not an aristocracy. . . .

Now one of two things is true; either a Republic is a desirable form of government, or else it is not. If it is, then we should have it, if it is not then we ought not to pretend that we have it. We ought, at least, to be true to our ideals, and the men of New York have, for the first time in their lives the rare opportunity, on the second day of next November, of making this state truly a part of a Republic. . . .

Now what is a Republic? Take your dictionary, encyclopedia, lexicon or anything else you like and look up the definition

137

and you will find that a Republic is a form of government in which the laws are enacted by representatives elected by the people. Now when did the people of New York ever elect their representatives? Never in the world. The men of New York have, and I grant you that men are people, admirable people, as far as they go, but they only go half way. There is still another half of the people who have not elected representatives, and you never read a definition of a Republic in which half of the people elect representatives to govern the whole of the people. That is an aristocracy and that is just what we are. We have been many kinds of aristocracies. We have been a hierarchy of church members, then an aristocracy of wealth, then an oligarchy of sex.

There are two old theories which are dying today. Dying hard but dying. One of them is dying on the plains of Flanders and the Mountains of Galicia and Austria and that is the theory of the divine right of kings. The other is dying here in the state of New York and Massachusetts and New Jersey and Pennsylvania and that is the divine right of sex. Neither of them had a foundation in reason, or justice or common sense. . . .

When I was speaking in North Dakota from an automobile with a great crowd and a great number of men gathered around, a man who had been sitting in front of a store whittling a stick called out to another man and asked if women get the vote will they go over to Germany and fight the Germans? I said, "Why no, . . . but if Germany should send an army of women over here, then we would show you what we would do. We would go down and meet them and say, 'Come on, let's go . . . talk this matter over.' It might grow wearisome but it would not be death."

Would it not be better if the heads of the governments in Europe had talked things over? What might have happened to the world if a dozen men had gotten together in Europe and settled the awful controversy which is today decimating the nations of Europe? . . .

No, we women do not want the ballot in order that we may fight, but we do want the ballot in order that we may help men to keep from fighting, whether it is in war or in peace; whether it is in the home or in the state, just as the home is not without the man, so the state is not without the woman, and you can no more build up homes without men than you can build up the state without women. We are needed everywhere where human life is. We are needed everywhere where human problems are to [be] solve[d] and men and women must go through this world together from the cradle to the grave, it is God's way and it is the fundamental principle of a Republican form of government.

☆

Woodrow Wilson

"The World Must Be Made Safe for Democracy"

Washington, D.C.
April 2, 1917

When a German submarine torpedoed the unarmed British passenger ship Lusitania *after it left New York in 1915, killing almost 1,200 people, the incident was handled diplomatically by President Woodrow Wilson, who had long worked for peace in Europe and wanted to keep the United States out of World War I. Then in March of 1917, Germany announced it would resume submarine warfare against even neutral nations, and began sinking American ships. President Wilson asked Congress to declare war on Germany.*

☆ ☆

I have called the Congress into extraordinary session because there are serious, very serious, choices of policy to be made, and made immediately, which it was neither right nor constitutionally permissible that I should assume the responsibility of making.

On the third of February last, I officially laid before you the extraordinary announcement of the Imperial German government that on and after the first day of February it was its purpose to put aside all restraints of law or of humanity and use its submarines to sink every vessel that sought to approach either the ports of Great Britain and Ireland, or the western coasts of Europe, or any of the ports controlled by the enemies of Germany within the Mediterranean. . . .

Vessels of every kind, whatever their flag, their character, their cargo, their destination, their errand, have been ruthlessly sent to the bottom without warning and without thought of help or mercy for those on board—the vessels of friendly neutrals along with those of belligerents. Even hospital ships . . . have been sunk with the same reckless lack of compassion or of principle. . . .

It is a war against all nations. American ships have been sunk, American lives taken, in ways which it has stirred us very deeply to learn of, but the ships and people of other neutral and friendly nations have been sunk and overwhelmed in the waters in the same way. There has been no discrimination. The challenge is to all mankind. Each nation must decide for itself how it will meet it. The choice we make for ourselves must be made with a moderation of counsel and a temperateness of judgment befitting our character and our motives as a nation. We must put excited feeling away. Our motive will not be revenge or the victorious assertion of the physical might of the nation, but only the vindication of right, of human right, of which we are only a single champion. . . .

With a profound sense of the solemn and even tragical character of the step I am taking, and of the grave responsibilities which it involves, but in unhesitating obedience to what I deem my constitutional duty, I advise that the Congress declare the recent course of the Imperial German government to be in fact nothing less than war against the government and people of the United States; that it formally accept the status of belligerent which has thus been thrust upon it; and that it take immediate steps not only to put the country in a more thorough state of defense, but also to exert all its power and employ all its resources to bring the government of the German Empire to terms and end the war. . . .

We have no quarrel with the German people. We have no feeling toward them but one of sympathy and friendship. It was not upon their impulse that their government acted in entering this war. It was not with their previous knowledge or approval. It was a war determined upon as wars used to be determined upon in the old, unhappy days when peoples were nowhere consulted by their rulers and wars were provoked and waged in the interest of dynasties or little groups of ambitious men who were accustomed to use their fellow men as pawns and tools. . . .

We are glad, now that we see the facts with no veil of false pretense about them, to fight thus for the ultimate peace of the world and for the liberation of its peoples, the German peoples included: for the rights of nations great and small and the privilege of men everywhere to choose their way of life and of obedience. The world must be made safe for democracy. Its peace must be planted upon the tested foundations of political liberty. We have no selfish ends to serve. We desire no conquest, no dominion. We seek no indemnities for ourselves, no material compensation for the sacrifices we shall freely make. We are but one of the champions of the rights of mankind. . . .

It is a distressing and oppressive duty, gentlemen of the Congress, which I have performed in thus addressing you. There are, it may be, many months of fiery trial and sacrifice ahead of us. It is a fearful thing to lead this great peaceful people into war, into the most terrible and disastrous of all wars, civilization itself seeming to be in the balance. But the right is more precious than peace, and we shall fight for the things which we have always carried nearest our hearts—for democracy, for the right of those who submit to authority to have a voice in their own governments, for the rights and liberties of small nations, for a universal dominion of right by such a concert of free peoples as shall bring peace and safety to all nations and make the world itself at last free. To such a task we can dedicate our lives and our fortunes, everything that we are and everything that we have, with the pride of those who know that the day has come when America is privileged to spend her blood and her might for the principles that gave her birth and happiness and the peace which she has treasured. God helping her, she can do no other.

Emma Goldman speaking from a car in 1914.

Emma Goldman

"First Make Democracy Safe in America"

New York City
July 9, 1917

Emma Goldman, born in Lithuania, immigrated to New York as a girl; there she lived the harsh life of the working poor. She became a dynamic speaker for the anarchist movement, which espoused extreme individual freedom and the abolition of government. When an anarchist assassinated President McKinley in 1901, Goldman was jailed, and she was arrested for advocating resistance to the draft in 1917. At her trial she explained at length her views against war and the nature of patriotism, and in 1919 she was deported to Russia along with other dissenters and antiwar agitators.

☆ ☆

Gentlemen of the jury, we respect your patriotism. We would not, if we could, have you change its meaning for yourself. But may there not be different kinds of patriotism as there are different kinds of liberty? I for one cannot believe that love of one's country must consist in blindness to its social faults, in deafness to its social discords, in inarticulation of its social wrongs. Neither can I believe that the mere accident of birth in a certain country or the mere scrap of a citizen's paper constitutes the love of country.

I know many people—I am one of them—who were not born here, nor have they applied for citizenship, and who yet love America with deeper passion and greater intensity than many natives whose patriotism manifests itself by pulling, kicking, and insulting those who do not rise when the national anthem is played. Our patriotism is that of the man who loves a woman with open eyes. He is enchanted by her beauty, yet he sees her faults. So we, too, who know America, love her beauty, her richness, her great possibilities; we love her mountains, her canyons, her forests, her Niagara, and her deserts—above all do we love the people that have produced her wealth, her artists who have created beauty, her great apostles who dream and work for liberty—but with the same passionate emotion we hate her superficiality, her cant, her corruption, her mad, unscrupulous worship at the altar of the Golden Calf.

We say that if America has entered the war to make the world safe for democracy, she must first make democracy safe in America. How else is the world to take America seriously, when democracy at home is daily being outraged, free speech suppressed, peaceable assemblies broken up by overbearing and brutal gangsters in uniform; when free press is curtailed and every independent opinion gagged. Verily, poor as we are in democracy, how can we give of it to the world? We further say that a democracy conceived in the military servitude of the masses, in their economic enslavement, and nurtured in their tears and blood, is not democracy at all. It is despotism—the cumulative result of a chain of abuses which, according to that dangerous document, the Declaration of Independence, the people have the right to overthrow. . . .

Admitting that [our] Manifesto contains the expression, "Resist conscription," may I ask you, is there only one kind of resistance? Is there only the resistance which means the gun, the bayonet, the bomb or flying machine? Is there not another kind of resistance? May not the people simply fold their hands and declare, "We will not fight when we do not believe in the necessity of war"? May not the people who believe in the repeal of the Conscription Law, because it is unconstitutional, express their opposition in word and by pen, in meetings and in other ways? . . .

Whatever your verdict, gentlemen, it cannot possibly affect the rising tide of discontent in this country against war which, despite all boasts, is a war for conquest and military power. Neither can it affect the ever increasing opposition to conscription which is a military and industrial yoke placed upon the necks of the American people. . . .

Your verdict may, of course, affect us temporarily, in a physical sense—it can have no effect whatever upon our spirit. For even if we were convicted and found guilty and the penalty were that we be placed against a wall and shot dead, I should nevertheless cry out with the great Luther: "Here I am and here I stand and I cannot do otherwise." . . .

I may remind you of two great Americans, undoubtedly not unknown to you, gentlemen of the jury; Ralph Waldo Emerson and Henry David Thoreau. When Thoreau was placed in prison for refusing to pay taxes [to support the Mexican War], he was visited by Ralph Waldo Emerson and Emerson said: "David, what are you doing in jail?" and Thoreau replied: "Ralph, what are you doing outside, when honest people are in jail for their ideals?"

Gentlemen of the jury, . . . whatever your decision, the struggle must go on. We are but the atoms in the incessant human struggle towards the light that shines in the darkness—the ideal of economic, political and spiritual liberation of mankind!

☆

Eugene V. Debs

"While There Is a Lower Class, I Am in It"

Cleveland, Ohio
September 14, 1918

Eugene Debs was a railroad worker and union organizer who ran three times for president, once from prison. He helped found the Socialist Party in the United States, in the hope of bettering people's lives through government ownership of industry. With the entry of the United States into World War I, laws such as the Espionage Act of 1917 restricted freedom of speech and punished disloyalty to the government. A pacifist, Debs was tried and found guilty for making antiwar statements and obstructing the draft. In a moving address to the court before he was sentenced to jail, Debs asserted his lifelong commitment to the underprivileged. President Harding had him released from prison in 1921.

☆ ☆

Your Honor, years ago I recognized my kinship with all living beings, and I made up my mind that I was not one bit better than the meanest on earth. I said then, and I say now, that while there is a lower class, I am in it; while there is a criminal element, I am of it; and while there is a soul in prison, I am not free.

I listened to all that was said in this court in support and justification of this prosecution, but my mind remains unchanged. I look upon the Espionage Law as a despotic enactment in flagrant conflict with democratic principles and with the spirit of free institutions. . . .

Your Honor, I have stated in this court that I am opposed to the social system in which we live; that I believe in a fundamental change—but if possible by peaceable and orderly means. . . .

Standing here this morning, I recall my boyhood. At fourteen I went to work in a railroad shop; at sixteen I was firing a freight engine on a railroad. I remember all the hardships and privations of that earlier day, and from that time until now my heart has been with the working class. I could have been in Congress long ago. I have preferred to go to prison. . . .

I am thinking this morning of the men in the mills and factories; of the men in the mines and on the railroads. I am thinking of the women who for a paltry wage are compelled to work out their barren lives; of the little children who in this system are robbed of their childhood and in their tender years are . . . forced into the industrial dungeons, there to feed the monster machines while they themselves are being starved and stunted, body and soul. I see them dwarfed and diseased and their little lives broken and blasted because in this high noon of our twentieth-century Christian civilization, money is still so much more important than the flesh and blood of childhood. In very truth gold is god today and rules with pitiless sway in the affairs of men. . . .

I believe, Your Honor, in common with all Socialists, that this nation ought to own and control its own industries. I believe, as all Socialists do, that all things that are jointly needed and used ought to be jointly owned—that industry, the basis our social life, instead of being the private property of the few and operated for their enrichment, ought to be the common property of all, democratically administered in the interest of all. . . .

I am opposing a social order in which it is possible for one man who does absolutely nothing that is useful to amass a fortune of hundreds of millions of dollars, while millions of men and women who work all the days of their lives secure barely enough for a wretched existence.

This order of things cannot always endure. I have registered my protest against it. I recognize the feebleness of my effort, but fortunately, I am not alone. There are multiplied thousands of others who, like myself, have come to realize that before we may truly enjoy the blessings of civilized life, we must reorganize society upon a mutual and cooperative basis; and to this end we have organized a great economic and political movement that spreads over the face of all the earth.

There are today upwards of sixty millions of Socialists, loyal, devoted adherents to this cause, regardless of nationality, race, creed, color, or sex. They are all making common cause. They are spreading with tireless energy the propaganda of the new social order. They are waiting, watching, and working hopefully through all the hours of the day and the night. They are still in a minority. But they have learned how to be patient and to bide their time. They feel—they know, indeed—that the time is coming, in spite of all opposition, all persecution, when this emancipating gospel will spread among all the peoples, and when this minority will become the triumphant majority and, sweeping into power, inaugurate the greatest social and economic change in history.

In that day we shall have the universal commonwealth—the harmonious cooperation of every nation with every other nation on earth. . . .

Your Honor, I ask no mercy and I plead for no immunity. I realize that finally the right must prevail. I never so clearly comprehended as now the great struggle between the powers of greed and exploitation on the one hand and upon the other the rising hosts of industrial freedom and social justice.

I can see the dawn of the better day for humanity. The people are awakening. In due time they will and must come to their own.

I am now prepared to receive your sentence.

Clarence Darrow (center), exhausted by the trial of Leopold and Loeb.

Clarence Darrow

In Defense of Leopold and Loeb

Chicago, Illinois
August 22, 1924

The celebrated Chicago attorney Clarence Darrow was most famous for his defense of John Scopes, a Tennessee biology teacher charged with illegally teaching Darwinism. But Darrow was also known for his opposition to the death penalty. In 1924, six years after the end of World War I, he defended Nathan Leopold and Richard Loeb, two Chicago teenagers from well-to-do families who were charged with killing another boy, apparently with the aim of committing the "perfect crime." The two boys were found guilty, but Darrow's eloquent twelve-hour plea for mercy saved them from the death sentence. By the end, the judge and most in the court were in tears.

☆ ☆

For four long years the civilized world was engaged in killing men. Christian against Christian, barbarian uniting with Christians to kill Christians; anything to kill. It was taught in every school, aye in the Sunday schools. The little children played at war. The toddling children on the street. Do you suppose this world has ever been the same since then? How long, Your Honor, will it take for the world to get back the humane emotions that were slowly growing before the war? How long will it take the calloused hearts of men before the scars of hatred and cruelty shall be removed?

We read of killing one hundred thousand men in a day. We read about it and we rejoiced in it—if it was the other fellows who were killed. We were fed on flesh and drank blood. Even down to the prattling babe. I need not tell Your Honor this, because you know; I need not tell you how many upright, honorable young boys have come into this court charged with murder, some saved and some sent to their death, boys who fought in this war and learned to place a cheap value on human life. You know it and I know it. These boys were brought up in it. The tales of death were in their homes, their playgrounds, their schools; they were in the newspapers that they read; it was a part of the common frenzy—what was a life? It was nothing. It was the least sacred thing in existence and these boys were trained to this cruelty.

It will take fifty years to wipe it out of the human heart, if ever. I know this, that after the Civil War in 1865, crimes of this sort increased, marvelously. No one needs to tell me that crime has no cause. It has as definite a cause as any other disease, and I know that out of the hatred and bitterness of the Civil War crime increased as America had never known it before. I know that growing out of the Napoleonic wars there was an era of crime such as Europe had never seen before. I know that Europe is going through the same experience today; I know it has followed every war; and I know it has influenced these boys so that life was not the same to them as it would have been if the world had not been made red with blood. I protest against the crimes and mistakes of society being visited upon them. All of us have a share in it. I have mine. I cannot tell and I shall never know how many words of mine might have given birth to cruelty in place of love and kindness and charity.

Your Honor knows that in this very court crimes of violence have increased growing out of the war. Not necessarily by those who fought but by those that learned that blood was cheap, and human life was cheap, and if the state could take it lightly why not the boy? . . .

The easy thing and the popular thing to do is to hang my clients. I know it. Men and women who do not think will applaud. The cruel and thoughtless will approve. It will be easy today; but in Chicago, and reaching out over the length and breadth of the land, more and more fathers and mothers, the humane, the kind, and the hopeful, who are gaining an understanding and asking questions not only about these poor boys, but about their own—these will join in no acclaim at the death of my clients. These would ask that the shedding of blood be stopped. . . .

I know the future is with me, and what I stand for here; not merely for the lives of these two unfortunate lads, but for all boys and all girls; for all of the young, and as far as possible, for all of the old. I am pleading for life, understanding, charity, kindness, and the infinite mercy that considers all. I am pleading that we overcome cruelty with kindness and hatred with love. I know the future is on my side. Your Honor stands between the past and the future. You may hang these boys; you may hang them by the neck until they are dead. But in doing it you will turn your face toward the past. In doing it you are making it harder for every other boy who in ignorance and darkness must grope his way through the mazes which only childhood knows. In doing it you will make it harder for unborn children. You may save them and make it easier for every child that sometime may stand where these boys stand. You will make it easier for every human being with an aspiration and a vision and a hope and a fate. I am pleading for the future; I am pleading for a time when hatred and cruelty will not control the hearts of men. When we can learn by reason and judgment and understanding and faith that all life is worth saving, and that mercy is the highest attribute of man.

Alfred E. Smith

"Anything Un-American Cannot Live in the Sunlight"

Oklahoma City, Oklahoma
September 20, 1928

The Governor of New York State and a member of the Roman Catholic church, Alfred E. Smith ran unsuccessfully as the Democratic candidate for president against the Republican Herbert Hoover in 1928. The United States had never had a Catholic president, and Smith addressed the question of prejudice against Catholics in a campaign speech in Oklahoma City.

☆ ☆

I feel that I owe it to the Democratic party to talk out plainly. If I had listened to the counselors that advised political expediency I would probably keep quiet, but I'm not by nature a quiet man.

I never keep anything to myself. I talk it out. And I feel I owe it, not only to the party, but I sincerely believe that I owe it to the country itself to drag this un-American propaganda out into the open.

Because this country, to my way of thinking, cannot be successful if it ever divides on sectarian lines. If there are any considerable number of our people that are going to listen to appeals to their passions and to their prejudice, if bigotry and intolerance and their sister vices are going to succeed, it is dangerous for the future life of the Republic; and the best way to kill anything un-American is to drag it out into the open, because anything un-American cannot live in the sunlight.

Where does all this propaganda come from? Who is paying for its distribution? . . .

Prior to the convention the grand dragon of the Realm of Arkansas wrote to one of the delegates from Arkansas, and in the letter he advised the delegate that he not vote for me in the national convention, and he put it on the ground of upholding American ideals against institutions as established by our forefathers. Now, can you think of any man or any group of men banded together in what they call the Ku Klux Klan, who profess to be 100 per cent Americans, and forget the great principle that Jefferson stood for, the equality of man, and forget that our forefathers in their wisdom, foreseeing probably such a sight as we look at today, wrote into the fundamental law of the country that at no time was religion to be regarded as a qualification for public office.

Just think of a man breathing the spirit of hatred against millions of his fellow citizens, proclaiming and subscribing at the same time to the doctrine of Jefferson, of Lincoln, of Roosevelt and of Wilson. Why, there is no greater mockery in this world today than the burning of the Cross, the emblem of faith, the emblem of salvation, the place upon which Christ Himself made the great sacrifice for all of mankind, by these people who are spreading this propaganda, while the Christ they are supposed to adore, love and venerate, during all of His lifetime on earth, taught the holy, sacred writ of brotherly love. . . .

Let me make myself perfectly clear. I do not want any Catholic in the United States of America to vote for me on the 6th of November because I am a Catholic. If any Catholic in this country believes that the welfare, the well-being, the prosperity, the growth and the expansion of the United States is best conserved and best promoted by the election of Hoover, I want him to vote for Hoover and not for me.

But, on the other hand, I have the right to say that any citizen of this country that believes I can promote its welfare, that I am capable of steering the ship of state safely through the next four years and then votes against me because of my religion, he is not a real, pure, genuine American.

☆
Franklin D. Roosevelt

"The Only Thing We Have to Fear Is Fear Itself"

Washington, D.C.
March 4, 1933

The 1929 crash of the stock market was followed by the almost decade-long Great Depression. Franklin D. Roosevelt was governor of New York when he was elected president in November of 1932 during the worst of the Depression. Almost one-third of workers were out of jobs. In his inaugural address, Roosevelt sought to calm the populace and announced his plans to get the country back on its feet. Within a few years, numerous programs of Roosevelt's New Deal were in place, including the Work Projects Administration, Social Security, and even school lunches.

☆ ☆

This is a day of national consecration, and I am certain that my fellow-Americans expect that on my induction into the Presidency I will address them with a candor and a decision which the present situation of our nation impels.

This is preeminently the time to speak the truth, the whole truth, frankly and boldly. Nor need we shrink from honestly facing conditions in our country today. This great nation will endure as it has endured, will revive and will prosper.

So first of all let me assert my firm belief that the only thing we have to fear is fear itself—nameless, unreasoning, unjustified terror which paralyzes needed efforts to convert retreat into advance.

In every dark hour of our national life a leadership of frankness and vigor has met with that understanding and support of the people themselves which is essential to victory. I am convinced that you will again give that support to leadership in these critical days.

In such a spirit on my part and on yours we face our common difficulties. They concern, thank God, only material things. Values have shrunken to fantastic levels; taxes have risen; our ability to pay has fallen; government of all kinds is faced by serious curtailment of income; the means of exchange are frozen in the currents of trade; the withered leaves of industrial enterprise lie on every side; farmers find no markets for their produce; the savings of many years in thousands of families are gone.

More important, a host of unemployed citizens face the grim problem of existence, and an equally great number toil with little return. Only a foolish optimist can deny the dark realities of the moment.

Yet our distress comes from no failure of substance. We are stricken by no plague of locusts. Compared with the perils which our forefathers conquered because they believed and were not afraid, we have still much to be thankful for. Nature still offers her bounty and human efforts have multiplied it. Plenty is at our doorstep, but a generous use of it languishes in the very sight of the supply.

Our greatest primary task is to put people to work. This is no unsolvable problem if we face it wisely and courageously.

It can be accomplished in part by direct recruiting by the government itself, treating the task as we would treat the emergency of a war, but at the same time, through this employment, accomplishing greatly needed projects to stimulate and reorganize the use of our natural resources. . . .

Finally, in our progress toward a resumption of work we require two safeguards against a return of the evils of the old order; there must be a strict supervision of all banking and credits and investments; there must be an end to speculation with other people's money, and there must be provision for an adequate but sound currency. . . .

We do not distrust the future of essential democracy. The

people of the United States have not failed. In their need they have registered a mandate that they want direct, vigorous action.

They have asked for discipline and direction under leadership. They have made me the present instrument of their wishes. In the spirit of the gift I take it.

In this dedication of a nation we humbly ask the blessing of God. May He protect each and every one of us! May He guide me in the days to come!

Lou Gehrig in the dugout on the last day he played for the New York Yankees.

Lou Gehrig

"The Luckiest Man on the Face of the Earth"

New York City
July 4, 1939

The legendary New York Yankee first baseman Lou Gehrig, nicknamed the Iron Horse, set a record that stood for over fifty years for playing the most consecutive games. He was forced to quit baseball in May of 1939 by a rare disease that crippled him and took his life in 1941. When Yankee Stadium held Lou Gehrig Day in tribute to the great player, Gehrig didn't plan to speak, but, choked with emotion and wiping back tears, he stepped to the microphone.

☆☆

Fans, for the past two weeks you have been reading about a bad break I got. Yet today I consider myself the luckiest man on the face of the earth. I have been in ballparks for seventeen years and have never received anything but kindness and encouragement from you fans.

Look at these grand men. Which of you wouldn't consider it the highlight of his career just to associate with them for even one day?

Sure, I'm lucky. Who wouldn't consider it an honor to have known Jacob Ruppert; also the builder of baseball's greatest empire, Ed Barow; to have spent six years with that wonderful little fellow Miller Huggins; then to have spent the next nine years with that outstanding leader, that smart student of psychology—the best manager in baseball today—Joe McCarthy!

Sure, I'm lucky. When the New York Giants, a team you would give your right arm to beat, and vice versa, sends you a gift, that's something! When everybody down to the groundskeepers and those boys in white coats remember you with trophies, that's something.

When you have a wonderful mother-in-law who takes sides with you in squabbles against her own daughter, that's something. When you have a father and mother who work all their lives so that you can have an education and build your body, it's a blessing! When you have a wife who has been a tower of strength and shown more courage than you dreamed existed, that's the finest I know.

So I close in saying that I might have had a tough break; but I have an awful lot to live for!

Harold Ickes

"What Constitutes an American?"

New York City
May 18, 1941

Before the bombing of Pearl Harbor brought the United States into World War II, the wisdom of becoming involved in another European war was under considerable debate. Harold Ickes, secretary of the interior under President Franklin D. Roosevelt, gave an address to a crowd of 100,000 on "I Am an American Day" in New York's Central Park in which he considered the many reasons for going to the aid of the British.

☆ ☆

What constitutes an American? Not color nor race nor religion. Not the pedigree of his family nor the place of his birth. Not the coincidence of his citizenship. Not his social status nor his bank account. Not his trade nor his profession. An American is one who loves justice and believes in the dignity of man. An American is one who will fight for his freedom and that of his neighbor. An American is one who will sacrifice prosperity, ease and security in order that he and his children may retain the rights of free men. An American is one in whose heart is engraved the immortal second sentence of the Declaration of Independence.

Americans have always known how to fight for their rights and their way of life. Americans are not afraid to fight. They fight joyously in a just cause.

We Americans know that freedom, like peace, is indivisible. We cannot retain our liberty if three-fourths of the world is enslaved. Brutality, injustice and slavery, if practiced as dictators would have them, universally and systematically, in the long run would destroy us as surely as a fire raging in our nearby neighbor's house would burn ours if we didn't help to put out his.

If we are to retain our freedom, we must do everything within our power to aid Britain. We must also do everything to restore to the conquered peoples their freedom. This means the Germans too.

Such a program, if you stop to think, is selfishness on our part. It is the sort of enlightened selfishness that makes the wheels of history go around. It is the sort of enlightened self-ishness that wins victories.

☆

Franklin D. Roosevelt

"A Date Which Will Live in Infamy"
Washington, D.C.
December 8, 1941

On December 7, 1941, while representatives of the Japanese government attended negotiations in Washington, the U.S. naval base at Pearl Harbor in Hawaii was bombed by Japanese forces without warning. Nineteen ships were sunk or damaged, nearly 200 planes were destroyed, and over 2,000 people were killed. Almost the entire U.S. Pacific fleet was destroyed. The next day, President Roosevelt asked Congress to declare war on Japan, and a few days later Germany and Italy declared war on the United States.

☆ ☆

Mr. Vice President, Mr. Speaker, members of the Senate and the House of Representatives: Yesterday, December 7, 1941—a date which will live in infamy—the United States of America was suddenly and deliberately attacked by naval and air forces of the empire of Japan.

The United States was at peace with that nation, and, at the solicitation of Japan, was still in conversation with its government and its Emperor looking toward the maintenance of peace in the Pacific.

Indeed, one hour after Japanese air squadrons had commenced bombing in the American island of Oahu the Japanese Ambassador to the United States and his colleague delivered to our Secretary of State a formal reply to a recent American message. And, while this reply stated that it seemed useless to continue the existing diplomatic negotiations, it contained no threat or hint of war or of armed attack.

It will be recorded that the distance of Hawaii from Japan makes it obvious that the attack was deliberately planned many days or even weeks ago. During the intervening time the Japanese Government has deliberately sought to deceive the United States by false statements and expressions of hope for continued peace.

The attack yesterday on the Hawaiian Islands has caused severe damage to American naval and military forces. I regret to tell you that very many American lives have been lost. In addition, American ships have been reported torpedoed on the high seas between San Francisco and Honolulu.

Yesterday the Japanese Government also launched an attack against Malaya.

Last night Japanese forces attacked Hong Kong.

Last night Japanese forces attacked Guam.

Last night Japanese forces attacked the Philippine Islands.

Last night the Japanese attacked Wake Island.

And this morning the Japanese attacked Midway Island.

Japan has therefore undertaken a surprise offensive extending throughout the Pacific area. The facts of yesterday and today speak for themselves. The people of the United States have already formed their opinions and well understand the implications to the very life and safety of our nation.

As Commander in Chief of the Army and Navy I have directed that all measures be taken for our defense.

Always will our whole nation remember the character of the onslaught against us.

No matter how long it may take us to overcome this premeditated invasion, the American people, in their righteous might, will win through to absolute victory.

I believe that I interpret the will of the Congress and of the people when I assert that we will not only defend ourselves to the uttermost but will make it very certain that this form of treachery shall never again endanger us.

Hostilities exist. There is no blinking at the fact that our people, our territory and our interests are in grave danger.

With confidence in our armed forces, with the unbounding

determination of our people, we will gain the inevitable triumph. So help us God.

I ask that the Congress declare that since the unprovoked and dastardly attack by Japan on Sunday, December 7, 1941, a state of war has existed between the United States and the Japanese Empire.

☆

Learned Hand

"The Spirit of Liberty"

New York City

May 21, 1944

Learned Hand, a federal judge in New York for over forty years, was so highly respected that he was known as the "tenth justice of the Supreme Court." The United States was in its third year of World War II when Judge Hand spoke on the spirit of liberty to a large crowd at "I Am an American Day" in Central Park, New York City.

☆ ☆

We have gathered here to affirm a faith, a faith in a common purpose, a common conviction, a common devotion. Some of us have chosen America as the land of our adoption; the rest have come from those who did the same. For this reason we have some right to consider ourselves a picked group, a group of those who had the courage to break from the past and brave the dangers and the loneliness of a strange land.

What was the object that nerved us, or those who went before us, to this choice? We sought liberty; freedom from oppression, freedom from want, freedom to be ourselves. This we then sought; this we now believe that we are by way of winning.

What do we mean when we say that first of all we seek liberty? I often wonder whether we do not rest our hopes too much upon constitutions, upon laws and upon courts. These are false hopes; believe me, these are false hopes. Liberty lies in the hearts of men and women; when it dies there, no constitution, no law, no court can save it; no constitution, no law, no court can even do much to help it. While it lies there it needs no constitution, no law, no court to save it.

And what is this liberty which must lie in the hearts of men and women? It is not the ruthless, the unbridled will; it is not freedom to do as one likes. That is the denial of liberty, and leads straight to its overthrow. A society in which men recognize no check upon their freedom soon becomes a society where freedom is the possession of only a savage few; as we have learned to our sorrow.

What, then, is the spirit of liberty? I cannot define it; I can only tell you my own faith. The spirit of liberty is the spirit which is not too sure that it is right; the spirit of liberty is the spirit which seeks to understand the minds of other men and women; the spirit of liberty is the spirit which weighs their interests alongside its own without bias; the spirit of liberty remembers that not even a sparrow falls to earth unheeded.

The spirit of liberty is the spirit of Him who, near two thousand years ago, taught mankind that lesson it has never learned, but has never quite forgotten; that there may be a kingdom where the least shall be heard and considered side by side with the greatest.

And now . . . in the spirit of that America for which our young men are at this moment fighting and dying; in that spirit of liberty and of America I ask you to rise and with me pledge our faith in the glorious destiny of our beloved country. I now ask you to raise your hands and repeat with me this pledge:

I pledge allegiance to the flag of the United States of America, and to the Republic for which it stands—one nation, indivisible, with liberty and justice for all.

General Eisenhower speaks with the troops before D-Day.

Dwight D. Eisenhower

"The Eyes of the World Are upon You"

England
June 6, 1944

General Dwight D. Eisenhower led the British and American allied forces as supreme commander of the D-Day invasion of Normandy to liberate France from the Nazis. As the invasion began, he addressed the troops by a broadcast secretly recorded beforehand. The crossing of the English Channel to France formed one of the greatest armadas ever seen, sending 175,000 men and over 5,000 ships to war from the coast of England. By late July, the Germans had begun retreating east, and Paris was liberated on August 25.

☆ ☆

Soldiers, sailors and airmen of the Allied Expeditionary Force!

You are about to embark upon the Great Crusade, toward which we have striven these many months. The eyes of the world are upon you. The hopes and prayers of liberty-loving people everywhere march with you. In company with our brave Allies and brothers-in-arms on other Fronts, you will bring about the destruction of the German war machine, the elimination of Nazi tyranny over oppressed peoples of Europe, and security for ourselves in a free world.

Your task will not be an easy one. Your enemy is well trained, well equipped and battle-hardened. He will fight savagely.

But this is the year 1944! Much has happened since the Nazi triumphs of 1940–41. The United Nations have inflicted upon the Germans great defeats, in open battle, man-to-man. Our air offensive has seriously reduced their strength in the air and their capacity to wage war on the ground. Our Home Fronts have given us an overwhelming superiority in weapons and munitions of war, and placed at our disposal great reserves of trained fighting men. The tide has turned! The free men of the world are marching together to Victory!

I have full confidence in your courage, devotion to duty and skill in battle. We will accept nothing less than full Victory.

Good Luck! And let us all beseech the blessing of Almighty God upon this great and noble undertaking.

Fala enjoys a drive with President Franklin D. Roosevelt on the grounds of his home at Hyde Park, New York.

Franklin D. Roosevelt

The Fala Address

Washington, D.C.
September 23, 1944

Campaigning for an unprecedented fourth term in office, President Roosevelt addressed the International Brotherhood of Teamsters at a dinner in September of 1944. He included in his remarks the popular little black Scottish terrier, Fala, who was his constant companion in the White House. Fala's full name was "Murray, the Outlaw of Falahill," named after a Roosevelt ancestor.

☆ ☆

These Republican leaders have not been content with attacks on me, or my wife, or on my sons. No, not content with that, they now include my little dog, Fala. Well, of course, I don't resent attacks, and my family doesn't resent attacks, but Fala does resent them. You know, Fala is Scotch, and being a Scottie, as soon as he learned that the Republican fiction writers in Congress and out [of Congress] had concocted a story that I had left him behind on the Aleutian Islands and had sent a destroyer back to find him—at a cost to the taxpayers of two or three, or eight or twenty million dollars—his Scotch soul was furious. He has not been the same dog since. I am accustomed to hearing malicious falsehoods about myself—such as that old, worm-eaten chestnut that I have represented myself as indispensable. But I think I have a right to resent, to object to libelous statements about my dog.

*General Douglas McArthur (center) wades through the surf to the beach
at Leyte on his return to the Philippines.*

Douglas MacArthur

"People of the Philippines: I Have Returned"

Leyte Beach, Philippines
October 20, 1944

*General Douglas MacArthur had served in the Philippines several times before
World War II and was devoted to the island country. When he was driven from
the Philippines by the Japanese in 1942, he pledged, "I shall return." Two years
later, he waded ashore with U.S. Army forces on the island of Leyte to liberate the
Philippines and fulfill his promise. With a small audience of Filipinos and U.S.
troops on the beach, MacArthur gave an address that the Signal Corps broadcast
across the country's airwaves.*

☆ ☆

People of the Philippines: I have returned. By the grace of
Almighty God our forces stand again on Philippine soil—
soil consecrated in the blood of our two peoples. We have

come, dedicated and committed, to the task of destroying every vestige of enemy control over your daily lives and of restoring, upon a foundation of indestructible strength, the liberties of your people.

At my side is your President, Sergio Osmena, worthy successor to that great patriot, Manuel Quezon, with members of his cabinet. The seat of your government is now therefore firmly re-established on Philippine soil.

The hour of your redemption is here. Your patriots have demonstrated an unswerving and resolute devotion to the principles of freedom that challenges the best that is written on the pages of human history. I now call upon your supreme effort that the enemy may know from the temper of an aroused and outraged people within that he has a force there to contend with no less violent than is the force committed from without.

Rally to me. Let the indomitable spirit of Bataan and Corregidor lead on. As the lines of battle roll forward to bring you within the zone of operations, rise and strike. Strike at every favorable opportunity. For your home and hearths, strike! For future generations of your sons and daughters, strike! In the name of your sacred dead, strike! Let no heart be faint. Let every arm be steeled. The guidance of divine God points the way. Follow in His Name to the Holy Grail of righteous victory.

Roland Gittelsohn

Eulogy at the Marine Corps Cemetery

Iwo Jima, Japan
March 26, 1945

Rabbi Roland Gittelsohn, a Jewish Marine Corps chaplain, ministered to soldiers in combat during the month-long World War II battle against Japan for the island of Iwo Jima. After Iwo Jima was won, he was asked to dedicate the Marine Corps Cemetery on the island. But because of objections to a joint service, separate services were held for Catholics, Protestants, and Jews. Three Christian chaplains attended Gittelsohn's service, where he gave the eulogy he had written for all, and they later circulated Gittelsohn's sermon to the troops. The sermon makes many allusions to the Gettysburg Address, President Lincoln's own dedication of a military cemetery.

This is perhaps the grimmest, and surely the holiest task we have faced since D-Day. Here before us lie the bodies of comrades and friends. Men who until yesterday or last week laughed with us, joked with us, trained with us. Men who were on the same ships with us, and went over the sides with us, as we prepared to hit the beaches of this island. Men who fought with us and feared with us. Somewhere in this plot of ground there may lie the man who could have discovered the cure for cancer. Under one of these Christian crosses, or beneath a Jewish Star of David, there may rest now a man who was destined to be a great prophet to find the way, perhaps, for all to live in plenty, with poverty and hardship for none. Now they lie here silently in this sacred soil, and we gather to consecrate this earth in their memory.

It is not easy to do so. Some of us have buried our closest friends here. We saw these men killed before our very eyes. Any one of us might have died in their places. Indeed, some of

173

us are alive and breathing at this very moment only because men who lie here beneath us had the courage and strength to give their lives for ours. To speak in memory of such men as these is not easy. Of them, too, can it be said with utter truth: "The world will little note nor long remember what we say here. It can never forget what they did here."

No, our poor power of speech can add nothing to what these men, and the other dead of our division who are not here, have already done. All that we can even hope to do is follow their example. To show the same selfless courage in peace that they did in war. To swear that, by the grace of God and the stubborn strength and power of human will, their sons and ours shall never suffer these pains again. These men have done their job well. They have paid the ghastly price of freedom. If that freedom be once again lost, as it was after the last war, the unforgivable blame will be ours, not theirs. So it be the living who are here to be dedicated and consecrated.

We dedicate ourselves, first, to live together in peace the way they fought and are buried in war. Here lie men who loved America because their ancestors, generations ago, helped in her founding, and other men who loved her with equal passion because they themselves or their own fathers escaped from oppression to her blessed shores. Here lie officers and men, Negroes and whites, rich men and poor . . . together. Here are Protestants, Catholics, and Jews . . . together. Here no man prefers another because of his faith or despises him because of his color. Here there are no quotas of how many from each group are admitted or allowed. Among these men there is no discrimination. No prejudice. No hatred. Theirs is the highest and purest democracy.

Any man among us the living who fails to understand that, will thereby betray those who lie here dead. Whoever of us lifts his hand in hate against a brother, or thinks himself superior to those who happen to be in the minority, makes of this ceremony and of the bloody sacrifice it commemorates, an empty, hollow mockery. To this, then, as our solemn, sacred duty, do we the living now dedicate ourselves: to the right of Protestants, Catholics, and Jews, of white men and Negroes alike, to enjoy the democracy for which all of them have here paid the price. . . .

Thus do we memorialize those who, having ceased living with us, now live within us. Thus do we consecrate ourselves, the living, to carry on the struggle they began. Too much blood has gone into this soil for us to let it lie barren. Too much pain and heartache have fertilized the earth on which we stand. We here solemnly swear: this shall not be in vain. Out of this, and from the suffering and sorrow of those who mourn this, will come—we promise—the birth of a new freedom for the sons of men everywhere. Amen

Albert Einstein serves as chairman of the Emergency Committee of Atomic Scientists, which was organized to promote nuclear disarmament.

Albert Einstein

To the United Nations

New York City
November 11, 1947

Albert Einstein was a German physicist who won the Nobel Prize for Physics in 1921. Because he was Jewish, he was forced to flee Germany when the Nazis came to power. He came to America, taught at Princeton University, and became a U.S. citizen. It was his urging of President Roosevelt to explore atomic energy for the production of weapons that led to the development of the atomic bomb used in World War II. After the war, Einstein lectured frequently to promote peace and world disarmament, as in this speech to representatives of the United Nations at a Foreign Press Association dinner.

☆ ☆

Everyone is aware of the difficult and menacing situation in which human society—shrunk into one community with a common fate—finds itself, but only a few act accordingly.

176

Most people go on living their everyday life: half frightened, half indifferent, they behold the ghostly tragicomedy that is being performed on the international stage before the eyes and ears of the world. But on that stage, on which the actors under the floodlights play their ordained parts, our fate of tomorrow, life or death of the nations, is being decided.

It would be different if the problem were not one of things made by man himself, such as the atomic bomb and other means of mass destruction equally menacing all peoples. It would be different, for instance, if an epidemic of bubonic plague were threatening the entire world. In such a case conscientious and expert persons would be brought together and they would work out an intelligent plan to combat the plague. After having reached agreement upon the right ways and means, they would submit their plan to the governments. Those would hardly raise serious objections but rather agree speedily on the measures to be taken. They certainly would never think of trying to handle the matter in such a way that their own nation would be spared whereas the next one would be decimated.

But could not our situation be compared to one of a menacing epidemic? People are unable to view this situation in its true light, for their eyes are blinded by passion. General fear and anxiety create hatred and aggressiveness. The adaptation to warlike aims and activities has corrupted the mentality of man; as a result, intelligent, objective, and humane thinking has hardly any effect and is even suspected and persecuted as unpatriotic.

There are, no doubt, in the opposite camps enough people of sound judgment and sense of justice who would be capable and eager to work out together a solution for the factual difficulties. But the efforts of such people are hampered by the fact that it is made impossible for them to come together for informal discussions. I am thinking of persons who are accustomed to the objective approach to a problem and who will not be confused by exaggerated nationalism or other passions.

This forced separation of the people of both camps I consider one of the major obstacles to the achievement of an acceptable solution of the burning problem of international security. . . .

We scientists believe that what we and our fellow men do or fail to do within the next few years will determine the fate of our civilization. And we consider it our task untiringly to explain this truth, to help people realize all that is at stake, and to work, not for appeasement, but for understanding and ultimate agreement between peoples and nations of different views.

Margaret Chase Smith

"The Four Horsemen of Calumny"

U.S. Senate, Washington, D.C.
June 1, 1950

Margaret Chase Smith, from Maine, was the sole woman serving in the Senate in 1950 when Senator Joseph McCarthy of Wisconsin began his crusade to uncover alleged communists among prominent Americans. Smith led a group of seven senators in presenting a Declaration of Conscience, which appealed to Congress to protect individual freedoms and to end the false and sensational accusations that became known as McCarthyism. Her speech introducing the Declaration was the first to condemn McCarthy's smear campaign. In 1954 the Senate finally censured him officially.

☆ ☆

Mr. President, I would like to speak briefly and simply about a serious national condition. It is a national feeling of fear and frustration that could result in national suicide and the end of everything that we Americans hold dear. . . .

I speak as briefly as possible because too much harm has already been done with irresponsible words of bitterness and selfish political opportunism. I speak as simply as possible because the issue is too great to be obscured by eloquence. I speak simply and briefly in the hope that my words will be taken to heart.

Mr. President, I speak as a Republican. I speak as a woman. I speak as a United States senator. I speak as an American.

The United States Senate has long enjoyed worldwide respect as the greatest deliberative body in the world. But recently that deliberative character has too often been debased to the level of a forum of hate and character assassination sheltered by the shield of congressional immunity.

It is ironical that we senators can in debate in the Senate, . . . verbally attack anyone else without restraint and with full protection, and yet we hold ourselves above the same type of criticism here on the Senate floor. Surely the United States Senate is big enough to take self-criticism and self-appraisal. Surely we should be able to take the same kind of character attacks that we "dish out" to outsiders.

I think that it is high time for the United States Senate and its members to do some real soul-searching and to weigh our consciences as to the manner in which we are performing our duty to the people of America and the manner in which we are using or abusing our individual powers and privileges.

I think it is high time that we remembered that we have sworn to uphold and defend the Constitution. I think it is high time that we remembered that the Constitution, as amended, speaks not only of the freedom of speech but also of trial by jury instead of trial by accusation.

Whether it be a criminal prosecution in court or a character prosecution in the Senate, there is little practical distinction when the life of a person has been ruined.

Those of us who shout the loudest about Americanism in making character assassinations are all too frequently those who, by our own words and acts, ignore some of the basic principles of Americanism—the right to criticize; the right to hold unpopular beliefs; the right to protest; the right of independent thought.

The exercise of these rights should not cost one single American citizen his reputation or his right to a livelihood, nor should he be in danger of losing his reputation or livelihood merely because he happens to know someone who holds unpopular beliefs. Who of us does not? Otherwise none of us could call our souls our own. Otherwise thought control would have set in.

The American people are sick and tired of being afraid to speak their minds lest they be politically smeared as Communists or Fascists by their opponents. Freedom of speech is not what it used to be in America. It has been so abused by some that it is not exercised by others.

The American people are sick and tired of seeing innocent people smeared and guilty people whitewashed. But there have been enough proved cases . . . to cause nationwide distrust and strong suspicion that there may be something to the unproved, sensational accusations. . . . Surely it is clear that this nation will continue to suffer so long as it is governed by the present ineffective Democratic administration.

Yet to displace it with a Republican regime embracing a philosophy that lacks political integrity or intellectual honesty would prove equally disastrous to the nation. The nation sorely needs a Republican victory. But I do not want to see the Republican party ride to political victory on the Four Horsemen of Calumny—fear, ignorance, bigotry, and smear. . . .

I do not want to see the Republican party win that way. While it might be a fleeting victory for the Republican party, it would be a more lasting defeat for the American people. Surely it would ultimately be suicide for the Republican party and two-party system that has protected our American liberties from the dictatorship of a one-party system. . . .

As an American, I am shocked at the way Republicans and Democrats alike are playing directly into the Communist design of "confuse, divide, and conquer." As an American, I do not want a Democratic administration whitewash or cover up any more than I want a Republican smear or witch-hunt.

As an American, I condemn a Republican Fascist just as much as I condemn a Democrat Communist. I condemn a Democrat Fascist just as much as I condemn a Republican Communist. They are equally dangerous to you and me and to our country. As an American, I want to see our nation recapture the strength and unity it once had when we fought the enemy instead of ourselves.

William Faulkner

"I Decline to Accept the End of Man"

Stockholm, Sweden
December 10, 1950

The prolific Mississippi-born writer William Faulkner, author of The Sound and the Fury, As I Lay Dying, *and many other noted works, was awarded the Nobel Prize for Literature in 1950. He addressed his acceptance speech to the young writers of the future and spoke of how they might be affected by fear of the atomic bomb. Only five years earlier, the use of the atomic bomb on Hiroshima had first compelled the world to consider the possibility of worldwide nuclear annihilation.*

☆ ☆

I feel that this award was not made to me as a man, but to my work—a life's work in the agony and sweat of the human spirit, not for glory and least of all for profit, but to create out of the materials of the human spirit something which did not exist before. So this award is only mine in trust.

It will not be difficult to find a dedication for the money part of it commensurate with the purpose and significance of its origin. But I would like to do the same with the acclaim too, by using this moment as a pinnacle from which I might be listened to by the young men and women already dedicated to the same anguish and travail, among whom is already that one who will someday stand here where I am standing.

Our tragedy today is a general and universal physical fear so long sustained by now that we can even bear it. There are no longer problems of the spirit. There is only the question: when will I be blown up? Because of this, the young man or woman writing today has forgotten the problems of the human heart in conflict with itself which alone can make good writing because only that is worth writing about, worth the agony and the sweat.

He must learn them again. He must teach himself that the basest of all things is to be afraid; and, teaching himself that, forget it forever, leaving no room in his workshop for anything but the old verities and truths of the heart, the old universal truths lacking which any story is ephemeral and doomed—love and honour and pity and pride and compassion and sacrifice. Until he does so, he labours under a curse. He writes not of love but of lust, of defeats in which nobody loses anything of value, of victories without hope, and, worst of all, without pity or compassion. His griefs grieve on no universal bones, leaving no scars. He writes not of the heart but of the glands.

Until he relearns these things, he will write as though he stood among and watched the end of man. I decline to accept the end of man. It is easy enough to say that man is immortal simply because he will endure; that when the last ding-dong of doom has clanged and faded from the last worthless rock hanging tideless in the last red and dying evening, that even then there will still be one more sound: that of his puny inexhaustible voice, still talking. I refuse to accept this.

I believe that man will not merely endure: he will prevail. He is immortal, not because he alone among creatures has an inexhaustible voice, but because he has a soul, a spirit capable of compassion and sacrifice and endurance. The poet's, the writer's, duty is to write about these things. It is his privilege to help man endure by lifting his heart, by reminding him of the courage and honour and hope and pride and compassion and pity and sacrifice which have been the glory of his past. The poet's voice need not merely be the record of man; it can be one of the props, the pillars, to help him endure and prevail.

Pearl Buck

Forbidden to Speak at
Cardozo High School Graduation

Washington, D.C.
January 26, 1951

Pearl Buck, author of The Good Earth, *won the 1938 Nobel Prize for Literature. Like many writers and artists, she came under suspicion of being a communist sympathizer during the Red Scare of the 1950s. Although she was invited to speak at the January 1951 mid-year graduation at the District of Columbia's Cardozo High School, a legally segregated all-black public school, the fearful school board barred her from attending. She sent to the students the speech she planned to give, and it was afterward published in* The Washington Post.

☆ ☆

It is a deep disappointment to me that I am not with you tonight. I had looked forward to the occasion as an opportunity when we might consider afresh, and together, the great ideals of our country, in order that we do our share toward preserving them in a threatening world.

That I am forbidden to be with you only makes the ideals of democracy the more valuable, the more important. . . . If anyone had told me a week ago that I could not stand before you tonight, I would not have believed it. That it has happened to you and to me makes me realize, as never before, that as long as the enemies of human freedom rule anywhere in the world, their evil influence creeps in everywhere.

It is true indeed and we must never forget it, that when other people lose their freedom, though they seem far from us, yet our freedom, too, is endangered. The first World War was called "a war to end all wars" and "a war for democracy" and yet its influence was to destroy to a certain degree freedom everywhere. In one country, Russia, then the weakest, amid the destruction and chaos that war always leaves, the hungry and desperate people gave themselves over to a revolution which has ended in the frightful tyranny which today threatens the world.

A second time this happened. After the Second World War again the weakest country, the most ruined by war and oppression, this time China, fell into the hands of the tyrants. Today under Communist governments, people do not dare even to speak their thoughts to each other. If you and I were in totalitarian countries today, I would not be allowed to speak to you either, because I stand for human freedom and equality, and these are the opposites of Communism as it appears in the world now. . . .

We who are still free must resolve with fresh courage to keep human freedom alive, and first of all in our own beloved country, in order that from here it may spread to a beleaguered world.

This courage may cost us much. The time may come, if we are not brave enough in the beginning, when it may cost us everything. What does courage mean? It means the determination to practice our ideals. We cannot keep our freedom unless we practice it. You and I, as individuals, must practice it, wherever we are. We cannot harbor prejudice against other persons. Race prejudice is not the only prejudice in our land. Within one group there is prejudice. We must not allow it in ourselves for any reason whatsoever, for to the degree we allow it, we deny human freedom. We must root out of ourselves the denial of freedom before we can fight for freedom in the world. . . .

Do not be discouraged by what has happened to you and to me. There are millions of people in our country who believe in our American ideals and practice them. Such people will be warned by what has happened to us, this incident which keeps me from speaking to you face to face, a small incident, really, affecting only one school and one person. But the news of it has already gone abroad. It is an incident tremendous in its significance, not that we are important, but it is important that such a thing could have happened here. That it did happen is a fact that we must use, too, in our own lives. Let us make it work for our ideals and not against them. Those who lose even a little freedom must be the ones to work with complete courage and all their strength for freedom, while there is yet time.

Let us thank God that ours is a country where there is yet time. We can still speak, if not in one place, then in another. We can still communicate with each other. We need not fear secret police—not yet. We can still trust family and friends. We do not walk solitary and in terror. We have courts of law which are still just, still ready to protect the individual and his rights. We have people brave enough to say what they think. We can still criticize our Government and each other—we can still make a little fun of each other's failings, and thank God for that, too. We still have freedom to laugh.

Already in totalitarian countries a man faces death if he criticizes his government. . . . You will find, as you go out into the world, that the great difference between the Communist and the democratic forms of government is that the Communist, like the Fascist, believes that any means are justified by the end. We know that this is false. The end itself, the good result for which we struggle, is lost if the means we use to attain it are unworthy. We cannot use oppression to gain freedom. Freedom is lost on the way. . . .

And how shall we keep our ideals alive?

Practice them—practice them! There is no other way. Practice them whether others do or not. Practice them the more earnestly because others do not. If one person fails, another must stand the more strong. Freedom is our birthright. Never forget that!

Charlotta Bass

"Let My People Go"

Chicago, Illinois
March 30, 1952

Charlotta Bass was a militant African American from Los Angeles who was active in many civil rights organizations. For forty years she published a crusading social reform newspaper, the California Eagle, *the oldest African American paper in the West. In 1952, she addressed the Progressive Party convention as candidate for vice president, and campaigned hard against the Republican vice presidential candidate, Richard Nixon, who won the election with Dwight D. Eisenhower.*

For the first time in the history of this nation a political party has chosen a Negro woman for the second highest office in the land.

It is a great honor to be chosen as a pioneer, and a great responsibility. . . .

I shall tell you how I came to stand here. I am a Negro woman. My people came before the Mayflower. I am more concerned with what is happening to my people in my country than war. We have lived through two wars and seen their promises turn to bitter ashes.

For forty years I have been a working editor and publisher of the oldest Negro newspaper in the West. During those forty years I stood on a watch tower watching the tide of racial hatred and bigotry rising against my people and against all people who believe the Constitution is something more than a piece of yellowed paper to be shut off in a glass cage in the archives.

I have stood watch over a home to protect a Negro family against the outrages of the Ku Klux Klan. And I have fought the brazen attempts to drive Negroes from their home under restrictive covenants. I have challenged the great corporations which extort huge profits from my people, and forced them to employ Negroes in their plants. I have stormed city councils and state legislatures and the halls of Congress demanding real representation for my people. . . .

One day the news flashed across the nation that a new party was born.

Here in this party was the political home for me and for my people. Here no one handed me a ready-made program from the back door. Here I could sit at the head of the table as a founding member, write my own program, a program for me and my people, that came from us. In that great founding convention in Philadelphia in 1948 we had crossed the Jordan. . . . Now perhaps I could retire. . . . I looked forward to a rest after forty years of struggle.

But could I retire when I saw that slavery had been abolished but not destroyed; that democracy had been won in World War I, but not for my people; that fascism had been wiped out in World War II, only to take roots in my own country where it blossomed and bloomed and sent forth its fruits to poison the land my people had fought to preserve! . . .

Where were the leaders of my nation—yes, my nation, for God knows my whole ambition is to see and make my nation the best in the world—where were these great leaders when these things happened?

To retire meant to leave this world to these people who carried oppression to Africa, to Asia, who made profits from oppression in my own land. To retire meant to leave the field to evil.

This is what we fight against. We fight to live. We want the $65 billion that goes for death to go to build a new life. Those billions could lift the wages of my people, give them jobs, give education and training and new hope to our youth, free our sharecroppers, build new hospitals and medical centers. The $8 billion being spent to rearm Europe and crush Asia could rehouse all my people living in the ghettos of Chicago and New York and every large city in the nation.

We fight that all people shall live. We fight to send our money to end colonialism for the colored peoples of the world, not to perpetuate it in Malan's South Africa, Churchill's Malaya, French Indo-China and the Middle East. . . .

I am stirred by the responsibility that you have put upon me. I am proud that I am the choice of the leaders of my own people and leaders of all those who understand how deeply the fight for peace is one and indivisible with the fight for Negro equality.

And I am impelled to accept this call, for it is the call of all my people and a call to my people. Frederick Douglass would rejoice, for he fought not only slavery but the oppression of women.

I make this pledge to my people, the dead and the living— to all Americans, black and white. I will not retire nor will I retreat, not one inch, so long as God gives me vision to see what is happening and strength to fight for the things I know are right. For I know that my kingdom, my people's kingdom, and the kingdom of all the peoples of all the world, is not beyond the skies, the moon and the stars, but right here at our feet.

I accept this great honor. I give you as my slogan in this campaign—"Let my people go."

The Nixon family (wife Pat, daughters Tricia, left, and Julie) play with their cocker spaniel, Checkers, at the beach in 1953.

Richard Nixon

The Checkers Speech

Los Angeles, California
September 23, 1952

Richard Nixon, then a senator from California, ran for vice president with Dwight D. Eisenhower in 1952. Just six weeks before the election, Nixon was accused of keeping campaign funds for his personal use. In refuting the accusation, he spoke of the gift to his daughters of a dog, Checkers, and the speech ever after was known as the "Checkers speech." The public loved it, and Nixon and Eisenhower won in a landslide.

☆ ☆

One other thing I probably should tell you, because if I don't they'll probably be saying this about me, too. We did get something, a gift, after the election. A man down in Texas heard Pat on the radio mention the fact that our two youngsters would like to have a dog. And, believe it or not, the day before we left on this campaign trip we got a message from Union Station in Baltimore saying they had a package for us.

We went down to get it. You know what it was? It was a little cocker spaniel dog in a crate that he'd sent all the way from Texas. Black and white spotted. And our little girl Tricia, the six-year old, named it Checkers. And you know, the kids, like all kids, love the dog; and I just want to say this right now, that regardless of what they say about it, we're gonna keep him.

Martin Luther King Jr.

"There Comes a Time When People Get Tired"

Montgomery, Alabama
December 5, 1955

Rosa Parks was an African American seamstress from Montgomery, Alabama, who was arrested for refusing to give up her seat on a bus to a white man. Within days, black community leaders organized a successful boycott of the city buses, which one year later resulted in a Supreme Court decision integrating the buses. The first day of the boycott, Martin Luther King Jr., a young preacher at a local church, was elected president of the Montgomery Improvement Association. It was then that King gave his first civil rights speech, at the end quoting from William Cowper's poem "The Negro's Complaint."

☆ ☆

We are here this evening for serious business. We are here in a general sense because first and foremost we are American citizens and we are determined to apply our citizenship to the fullness of its meaning. We are here also because of our love for democracy, because of our deep-seated belief that democracy transformed from thin paper to thick action is the greatest form of government on earth.

But we are here in a specific sense, because of the bus situation in Montgomery. We are here because we are determined to get the situation corrected. This situation is not at all new. The problem has existed over endless years. For many years now, Negroes in Montgomery and so many other areas have been inflicted with the paralysis of crippling fears on buses in our community. . . . Just the other day, just last Thursday to be exact, one of the finest citizens in Montgomery—not one of the finest Negro citizens, but one of the finest citizens in Montgomery—was taken from a bus and carried to jail and arrested because she refused to get up to give her seat to a white person. . . . And just because she refused to get up, she was arrested.

And you know, my friends, there comes a time when people get tired of being trampled over by the iron feet of oppression. There comes a time, my friends, when people get tired of being plunged across the abyss of humiliation, where they experience the bleakness of nagging despair. There comes a time when people get tired of being pushed out of the glittering sunlight of life's July and left standing amid the piercing chill of an alpine November. There comes a time.

We are here this evening because we're tired now. And I want to say that we are not here advocating violence. . . . My friends, don't let anybody make us feel that we are to be compared in our actions with the Ku Klux Klan or with the White Citizens Council. There will be no crosses burned at any bus stops in Montgomery. There will be no white persons pulled out of their homes and taken out on some distant road and lynched for not cooperating. . . .

We are not wrong in what we are doing. If we are wrong, the Supreme Court of this nation is wrong. If we are wrong, the Constitution of the United States is wrong. If we are wrong, God Almighty is wrong. If we are wrong, Jesus of Nazareth was merely a utopian dreamer that never came down to earth. . . .

As we prepare ourselves for what lies ahead, let us go out with a grim and bold determination that we are going to stick together. We are going to work together. Right here in Montgomery, when the history books are written in the future, somebody will have to say, "There lived a race of people, a black people, 'fleecy locks and black complexion,' a people who had the moral courage to stand up for their rights. And thereby they injected a new meaning into the veins of history and of civilization." And we're gonna do that. God grant that we will do it before it is too late.

☆
Langston Hughes

"On the Blacklist All Our Lives"

New York City
May 7, 1957

Langston Hughes was an African American poet and novelist who became known as the "Poet Laureate of Harlem." In 1957, with U.S. writers and artists of all colors blacklisted as suspected communist sympathizers, he addressed the National Assembly of Authors and Dramatists in New York City. Four years after his own interrogation by Senator Joseph McCarthy, Hughes described the difficulty that black writers had always faced in getting published in the United States.

☆ ☆

Bruce Catton spoke today of the writer's chance to be heard. My chance to be heard, as a Negro writer, is not so great as your chance, if you are white. I once approached the Play Service of the Dramatists Guild as to the handling of some of my plays. *No*, was the answer, they would not know where to place plays about Negro life. I once sent one of my best known short stories, before it came out in book form, to one of our oldest and foremost American magazines. The story was about racial violence in the South. It came back to me with a very brief little note saying the editor did not believe his readers wished to read about such things.

Another story of mine which did not concern race problems at all came back to me from one of our best known editors of anthologies of fiction with a letter praising the story but saying that he, the editor, could not tell if the characters were white or colored. Would I make them definitely Negro? Just a plain story about human beings from me was not up his alley, it seems. So before the word *man* I simply inserted *black*, and before the girl's name, the words *brownskin*—and the story

194

was accepted. Only a mild form of racial bias. But now let us come to something more serious.

Censorship, the Black List: Negro writers, just by being black, have been on the blacklist all our lives. Do you know that there are libraries in our country that will not stock a book by a Negro writer, not even as a gift? There are towns where Negro newspapers and magazines cannot be sold— except surreptitiously. There are American magazines that have *never* published anything by Negroes. There are film studios that have never hired a Negro writer. Censorship for us begins at the color line.

We have in America today about a dozen top flight, frequently published, and really good Negro writers. Do you not think it strange that of that dozen, at least half of them live abroad, far away from their people, their problems, and the sources of their material: . . . in Paris, . . . in Rome, . . . in Southern France, and . . . in Mexico.

Why? Because the stones thrown at Autherine Lucy at the University of Alabama are thrown at them, too. Because the shadow of Montgomery and the bombs under Rev. King's house, shadow them and shatter them, too. Because the body of little Emmett Till drowned in a Mississippi river and no one brought to justice, haunts them, too. One of the writers I've mentioned, when last I saw him before he went abroad, said to me, "I don't want my children to grow up in the shadow of Jim Crow."

And so let us end with children. And let us end with . . . a poem. It's about a child—a little colored child. I imagine her as being maybe six or seven years old. She grew up in the Deep South where our color lines are still legal. Then her family moved to a Northern or Western industrial city—one of those continual migrations of Negroes looking for a better town. There in this Northern city—maybe a place like Newark, New Jersey, or Omaha, Nebraska, or Oakland, California, the little girl goes one day to a carnival, and she sees the merry-go-round going around, and she wants to ride. But being a little colored child, and remembering the South, she doesn't know if she can ride or not. And if she can ride, where? So this is what she says:

> Where is the Jim Crow section
> On this merry-go-round,
> Mister, cause I want to ride?
> Down South where I come from
> White and colored
> Can't sit side by side.
> Down South on the train
> Down South on the train
> There's a Jim Crow car.
> On the bus we're put in the back—
> But there ain't no back
> To a merry-go-round:
> Where's the horse
> For a kid that's black?

☆

Roy Wilkins

"The Clock Will Not Be Turned Back"

San Francisco, California
November 1, 1957

As executive secretary of the National Association for the Advancement of Colored People, Roy Wilkins addressed the Commonwealth Club of California five weeks after mobs in Little Rock, Arkansas, attempted to prevent nine black students from entering Central High School. The defiant governor, Orval Forbus, called on National Guard troops to keep the students out, but President Eisenhower sent in federal troops to protect them. The school had been desegregated by a court order resulting from a 1954 landmark case, Brown v. Board of Education. *Wilkins spoke on the crisis facing not only black Americans, but the future of the United States during the Cold War.*

☆ ☆

It is no exaggeration, I think, to state that the situation presented by the resistance to the 1954 decision of the United States Supreme Court in the public school segregation cases is fully as grave as any which have come under the scrutiny and study of the Commonwealth Club. . . .

Little Rock brought the desegregation crisis sharply to the attention of the American people and the world. Here at home, it awakened many citizens for the first time to the ugly realities of a challenge to the very unity of our nation. Abroad, it dealt a stab in the back to American prestige as the leader of the free world and presented our totalitarian enemies with made-to-order propaganda for use among the very nations and peoples we need and must have on the side of democracy. . . .

The world cannot understand nor long respect a nation in which a governor calls out troops to bar little children from

197

school in defiance of the Supreme Court of the land, a nation in which mobs beat and kick and stone and spit upon those who happen not to be white. It asks: "Is this the vaunted democracy? Is this freedom, human dignity and equality of opportunity? Is this fair play? Is this better than Communism?" No, the assertion that Little Rock has damaged America abroad does not call for sneers. Our national security might well hang in the balance. . . .

The Negro citizens of our common country, a country they have sweated to build and died to defend, are determined that the verdict at Appomattox will not be renounced, that the clock will not be turned back, that they shall enjoy what is justly theirs. . . .

Their little children, begotten of parents of faith and courage, have shown by their fearlessness and their dignity that a people will not be denied their heritage. Complex as the problem is and hostile as the climate of opinion may be in certain areas, Negro Americans are determined to press for not only a beginning, but a middle and a final solution, in good faith and with American democratic speed.

The Negro position is clear. Three years of intimidation on the meanest and most brutal of levels have not broken their ranks or shaken their conviction.

What of the rest of our nation? It must make a decision for morality and legality and move in support of it, not merely for the good of the Negroes, but for the destiny of the nation itself.

Already I have indicated that this is a new and dangerous world. This cold war is a test of survival for the West. The Soviet sputnik, now silent and barely visible, casts a shadow not lightly to be brushed aside. Can we meet the challenge of Moscow in the sciences and in war with a country divided upon race and color? Can we afford to deny to any boy or girl the maximum of education, that education which may mean the difference between democratic life and totalitarian death? . . .

To deny our ability to achieve a just solution within the framework of our Declaration of Independence and our Bill of Rights is to deny the genius of Americans. To reject our moral precepts is to renounce our partnership with God in bringing the kingdom of righteousness into being here on earth.

We may falter and stumble, but we cannot fail.

John F. Kennedy delivers his inaugural address in 1961.

John F. Kennedy

"Ask What You Can Do for Your Country"

Washington, D.C.
January 20, 1961

At 43, President John Fitzgerald Kennedy was the youngest president ever elected. He was the first president born in the twentieth century, as well as the first Catholic one. His exciting and idealistic inaugural speech called Americans to serve their country, pledged the pursuit of peace and human rights and assistance to the world's poor, and warned aggressors that the United States would not tolerate interference in the Americas.

☆ ☆

We observe today not a victory of party but a celebration of freedom—symbolizing an end as well as a beginning, signifying renewal as well as change. For I have sworn before you and Almighty God the same solemn oath our forebears prescribed nearly a century and three-quarters ago.

The world is very different now. For man holds in his mortal hands the power to abolish all forms of human poverty and all forms of human life. And yet the same revolutionary beliefs for which our forebears fought are still at issue around the globe: the belief that the rights of man come not from the generosity of the state but from the hand of God.

We dare not forget today that we are the heirs of that first revolution. Let the word go forth from this time and place, to friend and foe alike, that the torch has been passed to a new generation of Americans—born in this century, tempered by war, disciplined by a hard and bitter peace, proud of our ancient heritage—and unwilling to witness or permit the slow undoing of those human rights to which this nation has always been committed, and to which we are committed today at home and around the world.

Let every nation know, whether it wishes us well or ill, that we shall pay any price, bear any burden, meet any hardship, support any friend, oppose any foe to assure the survival and the success of liberty.

This much we pledge—and more.

To those old allies whose cultural and spiritual origins we share, we pledge the loyalty of faithful friends. . . .

To those new states whom we welcome to the ranks of the free, we pledge our word that one form of colonial control shall not have passed away merely to be replaced by a far more iron tyranny. . . .

To those people in the huts and villages of half the globe struggling to break the bonds of mass misery, we pledge our best efforts to help them help themselves, for whatever period is required—not because the Communists may be doing it, not because we seek their votes, but because it is right. If a free society cannot help the many who are poor, it cannot save the few who are rich.

To our sister republics south of the border, we offer a special pledge: to convert our good words into good deeds—in a new alliance for progress—to assist free men and free governments in casting off the chains of poverty. But this peaceful revolution of hope cannot become the prey of hostile powers. Let all our neighbors know that we shall join with them to oppose aggression or subversion anywhere in the Americas. And let every other power know that this hemisphere intends to remain the master of its own house.

To that world assembly of sovereign states, the United Nations, our last best hope in an age where the instruments of war have far outpaced the instruments of peace, we renew our pledge of support—to prevent it from becoming merely a forum for invective, to strengthen its shield of the new and the weak, and to enlarge the area in which its writ may run.

Finally, to those nations who would make themselves our adversary, we offer not a pledge but a request: that both sides begin anew the quest for peace, before the dark powers of destruction unleashed by science engulf all humanity in planned or accidental self-destruction. . . .

So let us begin anew, remembering on both sides that civility is not a sign of weakness, and sincerity is always subject to proof. Let us never negotiate out of fear. But let us never fear to negotiate. . . .

Let both sides explore what problems unite us instead of belaboring those problems which divide us. . . .

And if a beachhead of cooperation may push back the jungle of suspicion, let both sides join in creating a new endeavor, not a new balance of power, but a new world of law, where the strong are just and the weak secure and the peace preserved.

All this will not be finished in the first one hundred days. Nor will it be finished in the first one thousand days, nor in the life of this administration, nor even perhaps in our lifetime on this planet. But let us begin.

In your hands, my fellow citizens, more than mine, will rest the final success or failure of our course. Since this country was founded, each generation of Americans has been summoned to give testimony to its national loyalty. The graves of young Americans who answered the call to service surround the globe.

Now the trumpet summons us again—not as a call to bear arms, though arms we need; not as a call to battle, though embattled we are—but a call to bear the burden of a long twilight struggle, year in and year out, "rejoicing in hope, patient in tribulation," a struggle against the common enemies of man: tyranny, poverty, disease, and war itself.

Can we forge against these enemies a grand and global alliance, north and south, east and west, that can assure a more fruitful life for all mankind? Will you join in that historic effort?

In the long history of the world, only a few generations have been granted the role of defending freedom in its hour of maximum danger. I do not shrink from this responsibility—I welcome it. I do not believe that any of us would exchange places with any other people or any other generation. The energy, the faith, the devotion which we bring to this endeavor will light our country and all who serve it—and the glow from that fire can truly light the world.

And so, my fellow Americans: Ask not what your country can do for you—ask what you can do for your country.

My fellow citizens of the world: Ask not what America will do for you, but what together we can do for the freedom of man.

Finally, whether you are citizens of America or citizens of the world, ask of us here the same high standards of strength and sacrifice which we ask of you. With a good conscience our only sure reward, with history the final judge of our deeds, let us go forth to lead the land we love, asking His blessing and His help, but knowing that here on earth God's work must truly be our own.

☆

Douglas MacArthur

"Duty, Honor, Country"

West Point, New York
May 12, 1962

The flamboyant World War II hero General Douglas MacArthur graduated from the U.S. Military Academy at West Point in 1903 and sixteen years later served as superintendent of the Academy. Late in life, at eighty-two, he returned to West Point to speak to the students, the Corps of Cadets.

☆☆

"Duty," "honor," "country"—those three hallowed words reverently dictate what you ought to be, what you can be, what you will be. They are your rallying points to build courage when courage seems to fail, to regain faith when there seems to be little cause for faith, to create hope when hope becomes forlorn. . . . They build your basic character. They mold you for your future roles as the custodians of the nation's defense. They make you strong enough to know when you are weak, and brave enough to face yourself when you are afraid.

They teach you to be proud and unbending in honest failure, but humble and gentle in success; not to substitute words for actions, nor to seek the path of comfort, but to face the stress and spur of difficulty and challenge; to learn to stand up in the storm, but to have compassion on those who fall; to master yourself before you seek to master others; to have a heart that is clean, a goal that is high; to learn to laugh, yet never forget how to weep; to reach into the future, yet never neglect the past; to be serious, yet never take yourself too seriously; to be modest so that you will remember the simplicity of true greatness, the open mind of true wisdom, the meekness of true strength. . . .

They teach you in this way to be an officer and a gentleman. . . .

You now face a new world, a world of change. . . . And through all this welter of change and development your mission remains fixed, determined, inviolable. It is to win our wars. Everything else in your professional career is but corollary to this vital dedication. All other public purpose, all other public projects, all other public needs, great or small, will find others for their accomplishments; but you are the ones who are trained to fight.

Yours is the profession of arms, the will to win, the sure knowledge that in war there is no substitute for victory; that if you lose, the nation will be destroyed; that the very obsession of your public service must be duty, honor, country. . . .

The long gray line has never failed us. Were you to do so, a million ghosts in olive drab, in brown khaki, in blue and gray, would rise from their white crosses, thundering those magic words: duty, honor, country.

This does not mean that you are warmongers. On the contrary, the soldier above all other people prays for peace, for he must suffer and bear the deepest wounds and scars of war. But always in our ears ring the ominous words of Plato, that wisest of all philosophers: "Only the dead have seen the end of war."

The shadows are lengthening for me. The twilight is here. . . . In my dreams I hear again the crash of guns, the rattle of musketry, the strange, mournful mutter of the battlefield. But in the evening of my memory I come back to West Point. Always there echoes and re-echoes: duty, honor, country.

Today marks my final roll call with you. But I want you to know that when I cross the river, my last conscious thoughts will be of the corps, and the corps, and the corps.

I bid you farewell.

☆

John F. Kennedy

"Let Them Come to Berlin"

Berlin, then West Germany
June 26, 1963

President Kennedy visited Berlin almost two years after the Berlin Wall was erected by order of the communist East German government. The wall divided Berlin in half and was built to prevent East Germans from escaping to the West. Speaking outdoors to a gigantic crowd of a million people, Kennedy's use of "I am a Berliner," spoken in German, had a tremendous effect on the audience, who roared his name in approval.

☆ ☆

Two thousand years ago the proudest boast was "Civis Romanus sum." Today, in the world of freedom, the proudest boast is "Ich bin ein Berliner."

There are many people in the world who really don't understand, or say they don't, what is the great issue between the free world and the Communist world. Let them come to Berlin. There are some who say that Communism is the wave of the future. Let them come to Berlin. And there are some who say in Europe and elsewhere we can work with the Communists. Let them come to Berlin. And there are even a few who say that it is true that Communism is an evil system, but it permits us to make economic progress. "Lass' sie nach Berlin kommen." Let them come to Berlin.

Freedom has many difficulties and democracy is not perfect, but we have never had to put a wall up to keep our people in, to prevent them from leaving us. I want to say, on behalf of my countrymen, who live many miles away on the other side of the Atlantic, who are far distant from you, that they take the greatest pride that they have been able to share with you, even from a distance, the story of the last eighteen years. I know of no town, no city, that has been besieged for eighteen years that still lives with the vitality and the force, and the hope and the determination of the city of West Berlin. While the wall is the most obvious and vivid demonstration of the failures of the Communist system, for all the world to see, we take no satisfaction in it, for it is an offense not only against history but an offense against humanity, separating families, dividing husbands and wives and brothers and sisters, and dividing a people who wish to be joined together.

What is true of this city is true of Germany—real, lasting peace in Europe can never be assured as long as one German out of four is denied the elementary right of free men, and that is to make a free choice. In eighteen years of peace and good faith, this generation of Germans has earned the right to be free, including the right to unite their families and their nation in lasting peace, with good will to all people. You live in a defended island of freedom, but your life is part of the main. So let me ask you, as I close, to lift your eyes beyond the dangers of today, to the hopes of tomorrow, beyond the freedom merely of this city of Berlin, or your country of Germany, to the advance of freedom everywhere, beyond the wall to the day of peace with justice, beyond yourselves and ourselves to all mankind.

Freedom is indivisible, and when one man is enslaved, all are not free. When all are free, then we can look forward to that day when this city will be joined as one—and this country, and this great continent of Europe—in a peaceful and hopeful globe. When that day finally comes, as it will, the people of West Berlin can take sober satisfaction in the fact that they were in the front lines for almost two decades.

All free men, wherever they may live, are citizens of Berlin, and, therefore, as a free man, I take pride in the words "Ich bin ein Berliner."

Martin Luther King Jr. delivers the "I Have a Dream" speech.

Martin Luther King Jr.

"I Have a Dream"

Washington, D.C.
August 28, 1963

Two months after President Kennedy introduced new civil rights legislation in Congress, the time seemed right for black civil rights leaders to demonstrate the depth of support they possessed among American citizens. Martin Luther King, along with other black leaders and Christian and Jewish religious leaders, organized the great March on Washington. A quarter of a million people, a fifth of them white, marched peacefully from the Washington Monument to the Lincoln Memorial, where King delivered his best-known speech. The celebrated last half was not planned by King, but came to him as a torrent of inspiration when he reached the end of his written remarks.

I say to you today, my friends, that in spite of the difficulties and frustrations of the moment I still have a dream. It is a dream deeply rooted in the American dream.

I have a dream that one day this nation will rise up and live out the true meaning of its creed: "We hold these truths to be self-evident; that all men are created equal."

I have a dream that one day on the red hills of Georgia the sons of former slaves and the sons of former slave owners will be able to sit down together at the table of brotherhood.

I have a dream that one day even the state of Mississippi, a desert state sweltering with the heat of injustice and oppression, will be transformed into an oasis of freedom and justice.

I have a dream that my four little children will one day live in a nation where they will not be judged by the color of their skin but by the content of their character.

I have a dream today.

I have a dream that one day the state of Alabama, whose governor's lips are presently dripping with the words of interposition and nullification, will be transformed into a situation where little black boys and black girls will be able to join hands with little white boys and white girls and walk together as sisters and brothers.

I have a dream today.

I have a dream that one day every valley shall be exalted, every hill and mountain shall be made low, the rough places will be made plains, and the crooked places will be made straight, and the glory of the Lord shall be revealed, and all flesh shall see it together.

This is our hope. This is the faith with which I return to the South. With this faith we will be able to hew out of the mountain of despair a stone of hope. With this faith we will be able to transform the jangling discords of our nation into a beautiful symphony of brotherhood. With this faith we will be able to work together, to pray together, to struggle together, to go to jail together, to stand up for freedom together, knowing that we will be free one day.

This will be the day when all of God's children will be able to sing with new meaning, "My country 'tis of thee, sweet land of liberty, of thee I sing. Land where my fathers died, land of the pilgrim's pride, from every mountainside, let freedom ring."

And if America is to be a great nation this must become true. So let freedom ring from the prodigious hilltops of New Hampshire. Let freedom ring from the mighty mountains of New York. Let freedom ring from the heightening Alleghenies of Pennsylvania!

Let freedom ring from the snowcapped Rockies of Colorado!

Let freedom ring from the curvaceous peaks of California!

But not only that; let freedom ring from Stone Mountain of Georgia!

Let freedom ring from Lookout Mountain of Tennessee!

Let freedom ring from every hill and molehill of Mississippi. From every mountainside, let freedom ring.

When we let freedom ring, when we let it ring from every village and every hamlet, from every state and every city, we will be able to speed up that day when all of God's children, black men and white men, Jews and Gentiles, Protestants and Catholics, will be able to join hands and sing in the words of the old Negro spiritual, "Free at last! Free at last! Thank God Almighty, we are free at last!"

Charles B. Morgan Jr.

"Four Little Girls Were Killed"

Birmingham, Alabama
September 16, 1963

Segregation was rigidly enforced in Birmingham, Alabama, in 1963. The city police used police dogs and water cannons against people protesting segregation, and as many as 2,000 demonstrators were thrown in jail in one day. On Sunday, September 15, four young African American girls attending church were killed by a bomb. The event shocked the nation. A day later, white Birmingham lawyer Charles Morgan Jr. addressed the city's Young Businessman's Club.

☆ ☆

Four little girls were killed in Birmingham yesterday.

A mad, remorseful worried community asks, "Who did it? Who threw that bomb? Was it a Negro or a white?" The answer should be, "We all did it." Every last one of us is condemned for that crime and the bombing before it and a decade ago. We all did it.

A short time later, white policemen kill a Negro and wound another. A few hours later, two young men on a motorbike shoot and kill a Negro child. Fires break out, and, in Montgomery, white youths assault Negroes.

And all across Alabama, an angry, guilty people cry out their mocking shouts of indignity and say they wonder "Why?" "Who?" Everyone then "deplores" the "dastardly" act.

But you know the "who" of "Who did it" is really rather simple. The "who" is every little individual who talks about the "niggers" and spreads the seeds of his hate to his neighbor and his son. The jokester, the crude oaf whose racial jokes rock the party with laughter.

The "who" is every governor who ever shouted for lawlessness and became a law violator.

It is every senator and every representative who in the halls of Congress stands and with mock humility tells the world that things back home aren't really like they are.

It is courts that move ever so slowly, and newspapers that timorously defend the law.

It is all the Christians and all their ministers who spoke too late in anguished cries against violence. It is the coward in each of us who clucks admonitions.

We have 10 years of lawless preachments, 10 years of criticism of law, of courts, of our fellow man, a decade of telling school children the opposite of what the civics books say.

We are a mass of intolerance and bigotry and stand indicted before our young. We are cursed by the failure of each of us to accept responsibility, by our defense of an already dead institution.

Yesterday while Birmingham, which prides itself on the number of its churches, was attending worship services, a bomb went off and an all-white police force moved into action, a police force which has been praised by city officials and others at least once a day for a month or so. A police force which has solved no bombings. A police force which many Negroes feel is perpetrating the very evils we decry. . . .

Birmingham is the only city in America where the police chief and the sheriff in the school crisis had to call our local ministers together to tell them to do their duty. The ministers of Birmingham who have done so little for Christianity call for prayer at high noon in a city of lawlessness, and in the same breath, speak of our city's "image." . . .

Those four little Negro girls were human beings. They have their 14 years in a leaderless city; a city where no one accepts responsibility; where everybody wants to blame somebody else. A city with a reward fund which grew like Topsy as a sort of sacrificial offering, a balm for the conscience of the "good people". . . .

Birmingham is a city . . . where four little Negro girls can be born into a second-class school system, live a segregated life, ghettoed into their own little neighborhoods, restricted to Negro churches, destined to ride in Negro ambulances, to Negro wards of hospitals or to a Negro cemetery. Local papers, on their front and editorial pages, call for order and then exclude their names from obituary columns.

And, who is really guilty? Each of us. Each citizen who has not consciously attempted to bring about peaceful compliance with the decisions of the Supreme Court of the United States, every citizen and every school board member and school-teacher and principal and businessman and judge and lawyer who has corrupted the minds of our youth; every person in this community who has in any way contributed during the past several years to the popularity of hatred, is at least as guilty, or more so, than the demented fool who threw that bomb.

What's it like living in Birmingham? No one ever really has known and no one will until this city becomes part of the United States.

Birmingham is not a dying city; it is dead.

Earl Warren

Eulogy for President John F. Kennedy

Capitol Rotunda, Washington, D.C.
November 24, 1963

Earl Warren was appointed chief justice of the Supreme Court by President Eisenhower in 1953. One of his most important decisions was the 1954 landmark case Brown v. Board of Education, *which declared segregated schools unconstitutional. When President Kennedy was shot and killed in Dallas, Texas, Justice Warren was appointed to lead the commission that investigated the assassination. Two days after the death of the president, Warren gave this eulogy in the Capitol rotunda, where Kennedy's body lay in state.*

☆ ☆

There are few events in our national life that so unite Americans and so touch the hearts of all of us as the passing of a President of the United States.

There is nothing that adds shock to our sadness more than the assassination of our leader, chosen as he is to embody the ideals of our people, the faith we have in our institutions, and our belief in the Fatherhood of God and the brotherhood of man. Such misfortunes have befallen the Nation on other occasions, but never more shockingly than two days ago. We are saddened; we are stunned; we are perplexed.

John Fitzgerald Kennedy—a great and good President, the friend of all people of good will; a believer in the dignity and equality of all human beings; a fighter for justice; an apostle of peace—has been snatched from our midst by the bullet of an assassin.

What moved some misguided wretch to do this horrible deed may never be known to us, but we do know that such

214

acts are commonly stimulated by forces of hatred and malevolence such as today are eating their way into the blood stream of American life. What a price we pay for this fanaticism!

It has been said that the only thing we learn from history is that we do not learn. But surely we can learn if we have the will to do so. Surely there is a lesson to be learned from this tragic event.

If we really love this country; if we truly love justice and mercy; if we fervently want to make this Nation better for those who are to follow us, we can at least abjure the hatred that consumes people, the false accusations that divide us and the bitterness that begets violence. Is it too much to hope that the martyrdom of our beloved President might even soften the hearts of those who would themselves recoil from assassination, but who do not shrink from spreading the venom which kindles thoughts of it in others?

Our Nation is bereaved. The whole world is poorer because of his loss. But we can all be better Americans because John Fitzgerald Kennedy has passed our way; because he has been our chosen leader at a time in history when his character, his vision and his quiet courage have enabled him to chart for us a safe course through the shoals of treacherous seas that encompass the world.

And now that he is relieved of the almost superhuman burdens we imposed on him, may he rest in peace.

☆

Malcolm X

"The Ballot or the Bullet"

New York City
March 22, 1964

Malcolm X was a controversial minister of the Nation of Islam, an American Muslim sect, who as a young man gave up his "slave name" of Malcolm Little. He was outspoken on the subject of black separatism and black nationalism, and he delivered this speech several times in Harlem in the year before he was assassinated by members of the Nation of Islam. Toward the end of his life, after visiting Mecca and traveling in Africa, Malcolm converted to mainstream Sunni Islam and softened his position on white people.

☆ ☆

Brothers and sisters and friends—

This afternoon we want to talk about the ballot or the bullet. The ballot or the bullet explains itself. But before we get into it, I would like to clarify some things. . . . about black nationalism.

The political philosophy of black nationalism only means that the black man should control the politics and the politicians in his own community. The time when white people can come in our community and get us to vote for them so that they can be our political leaders and tell us what to do and what not to do is long gone. . . .

The economic philosophy of black nationalism only means that we should own and operate and control the economy of our community. You can't open up a black store in a white community—white men won't even patronize it, and they're not wrong. They've got sense enough to look out for themselves. It's you who don't have sense enough to look out for yourselves. . . .

When you spend your dollar out of the community in which you live, the community in which you spend your money becomes richer and richer. The community out of which you take your money becomes poorer and poorer. And then what happens? The community in which you live becomes a slum. It becomes a ghetto. The conditions become run-down, and then you have the audacity to complain about poor housing and a run-down community. Why, you run it down yourselves when you take your dollar out. . . .

So our people not only have to be re-educated to the importance of supporting black business but the black man himself has to be made aware of the importance of going into business. What we will be doing is developing a situation wherein we will actually be able to create employment for the people in the community. . . . Any time you have to rely upon your enemies for a job you're in bad shape.

When we look at other parts of this earth upon which we live, we find that black, brown, red and yellow people in Africa and Asia are getting their independence. They're not getting it by singing "We shall overcome." No, they're getting it through nationalism. . . .

So it's time to wake up. It's got to be the ballot or the bullet. The ballot or the bullet. If you're afraid to use an expression like that, you should get on out of the country; you should get back in the cotton patch; you should get back in the alley.

When this country here was first being founded, there were thirteen colonies. The whites were colonized. They were fed up with this taxation without representation. So some of them stood up and said, "Liberty or death." Look, I went to a white school over here in Mason, Michigan. The white man made the mistake of lettin' me read his history books. He made the mistake of teaching me that Patrick Henry was a patriot. And George Washington—wasn't nothin' nonviolent about Old Pat or George Washington. "Liberty or death" was what brought about the freedom of whites in this country from the English. . . .

And here you have 22 million Afro-Americans, black people today, catchin' more hell than Patrick Henry ever saw. And I'm here to tell you in case you don't know, that you've got a new, a new generation of black people in this country, who don't care anything *whatsoever* about odds. They don't want to hear you old Uncle-Tom-handkerchief-heads talking about the odds.

America today finds herself in a unique situation. Historically, revolutions are bloody. Oh, yes, they are. They haven't ever had a bloodless revolution or a non-violent revolution. That don't happen even in Hollywood. You don't have a revolution in which you love your enemy. . . . But America is in a unique position. She's the only country in history in a position actually to become involved in a bloodless revolution. All she's got to do is give to the black man in this country everything that's due him. Everything. . . .

So it's the ballot or the bullet. Today our people can see that we're faced with a government conspiracy. The Senators who are filibustering concerning your and my rights, that's the government. Don't say it's Southern Senators. This is the government. . . . As long as you fight it on the level of civil rights, you're under Uncle Sam's jurisdiction. You're going to his court expecting him to correct the problem. He created the problem. He's the criminal. You don't take your case to the criminal. You take your criminal to court.

When the government of South Africa began to trample upon the human rights of the people of South Africa, they were taken to the U.N. When the government of Portugal began to trample upon the rights of our brothers and sisters in Angola, it was taken before the U.N. . . . Now, you tell me, how can the plight of everybody on this earth reach the halls of the U.N., and yet you have 22 million Afro-Americans whose churches are being bombed? Whose little girls are being murdered. Whose leaders are being shot down in broad daylight. Now, you tell me, why the leaders of this struggle have never taken it before the United Nations?

So, our next move is to expand the civil rights struggle to the level of human rights, take it into the United Nations, where our African brothers can throw their weight on our side, where our Asian brothers can throw their weight on our side, where our Latin-American brothers can throw their weight on our side, and where 800 million Chinese are sitting there, waiting to throw their weight on our side. And let the world see that Uncle Sam is guilty of violating the human rights of 22 million Afro-Americans and still has the audacity or the nerve to stand up and represent himself as the leader of the free world.

Let the world know how bloody his hands are. Let the world know the hypocrisy that's practiced over here. . . . It'll be the ballot or it'll be the bullet. It'll be liberty or it'll be death. And if you're not ready to pay that price, don't use the world freedom in your vocabulary.

Barry Goldwater delivering his acceptance speech at the 1964 Republican Convention.

Barry Goldwater

"Extremism in the Defense of Liberty Is No Vice"

San Francisco, California
July 16, 1964

The war against communist forces in Korea, the Cuban missile crisis of 1962, and the accelerating Vietnam War all kept Americans fearful and uncertain during the Cold War. Nikita Khrushchev, premier of the Soviet Union and head of the Communist party, had announced "We will bury you" to the West. At the Republican National Convention in 1964, conservative Senator Barry Goldwater accepted the nomination to run against President Johnson, who was up for reelection. But Goldwater's rousing anti-communist speech did not prevent his defeat.

☆ ☆

I accept your nomination with a deep sense of humility. I accept, too, the responsibility that goes with it. . . .

In this world no person, no party can guarantee anything, but what we can do and what we shall do is to deserve victory, and victory will be ours. The good Lord raised this mighty republic to be a home for the brave and to flourish as the land of the free—not to stagnate in the swampland of collectivism, not to cringe before the bully of communism. . . .

During four, futile years the administration which we shall replace has distorted and lost that faith. It has talked and talked and talked the words of freedom, but it has failed and failed and failed in the works of freedom.

Now failure cements the wall of shame in Berlin; failures blot the sands of shame at the Bay of Pigs; failures marked the slow death of freedom in Laos; failures infest the jungles of Vietnam; and failures haunt the houses of our once great alliances and undermine the greatest bulwark ever erected by free nations, the NATO community.

Failures proclaim lost leadership, obscure purpose, weakening wills, and the risk of inciting our sworn enemies to new aggressions and to new excesses. . . .

I needn't remind you—but I will—that it's been during Democratic years that our strength to deter war has been stilled and even gone into a planned decline. It has been during Democratic years that we have weakly stumbled into conflicts, timidly refusing to draw our own lines against aggression, deceitfully refusing to tell even our people of our full participation and tragically letting our finest men die on battlefields unmarked by purpose, unmarked by pride or the prospect of victory.

Yesterday it was Korea; tonight it is Vietnam. Make no bones of this. Don't try to sweep this under the rug. We are at war in Vietnam. And yet the president, who is the commander in chief of our forces, refuses to say—refuses to say, mind you—whether or not the objective over there is victory, and his secretary of defense continues to mislead and misinform the American people, and enough of it has gone by.

And I needn't remind you—but I will—it has been during Democratic years that a billion persons were cast into communist captivity and their fate cynically sealed. . . .

Now, the Republican cause demands that we brand communism as the principal disturber of peace in the world today. Indeed, we should brand it as the only significant disturber of the peace. And we must make clear that until its goals of conquest are absolutely renounced and its relations with all nations tempered, communism and the governments it now controls are enemies of every man on earth who is or wants to be free.

We can keep the peace only if we remain vigilant and strong. Only if we keep our eyes open and keep our guard up can we prevent war. . . . This is a party for free men, not for blind followers and not for conformists. In 1858 Lincoln said of the Republican Party that it was composed of "strange, discordant, and even hostile elements." Yet all of the elements agreed on one paramount objective: to arrest the progress of slavery and place it in the course of ultimate extinction.

Today, as then, . . . the task of preserving and enlarging freedom at home, and of safeguarding it from the forces of tyranny abroad, is enough to challenge all our resources and to require all our strength. . . .

I would remind you that extremism in the defense of liberty is no vice! And let me remind you also that moderation in the pursuit of justice is no virtue! . . .

Our Republican cause is to free our people and light the way for liberty throughout the world. Ours is a very human cause for very humane goals. This party, its good people, and its unquestionable devotion to freedom will not fulfill the purposes of this campaign which we launch here now until our cause has won the day, inspired the world, and shown the way to a tomorrow worthy of all our yesteryears.

Mario Savio

"History Has Not Ended"

Berkeley, California
December 2, 1964

When the University of California at Berkeley banned students from political activity on campus, they fought back with the nonviolent methods of the civil rights movement. A twenty-one-year-old philosophy student named Mario Savio became the spokesman for the Free Speech Movement, one of the first of many student movements across the nation. As one thousand students staged a sit-in of the Sproul Hall administration building, he addressed the press on his position against the university. A week later they won the right to campus activism.

☆ ☆

Last summer I went to Mississippi to join the struggle there for civil rights. This fall I am engaged in another phase of the same struggle, this time in Berkeley. The two battlefields may seem quite different to some observers, but this is not the case. The same rights are at stake in both places—the right to participate as citizens in democratic society and the right to due process of law. Further, it is a struggle against the same enemy. In Mississippi an autocratic and powerful minority rules, through organized violence, to suppress the vast, virtually powerless majority. In California, the privileged minority manipulates the university bureaucracy to suppress the students' political expression. . . .

In our free-speech fight at the University of California, we have come up against what may emerge as the greatest problem of our nation—depersonalized, unresponsive bureaucracy. We have encountered the organized status quo in Mississippi, but it is the same in Berkeley. . . . In September, to get the attention of this bureaucracy which had issued arbitrary edicts suppressing student political expression and refused to discuss its action, we held a sit-in on the campus. . . .

The things we are asking for in our civil-rights protests have a deceptively quaint ring. We are asking for the due process of law. We are asking for our actions to be judged by committees of our peers. We are asking that regulations ought to be considered as arrived at legitimately only from the consensus of the governed. These phrases are all pretty old, but they are not being taken seriously in America today, nor are they being taken seriously on the Berkeley campus.

The university is the place where people begin seriously to question the conditions of their existence and raise the issue of whether they can be committed to the society they have been born into. After a long period of apathy during the fifties, students have begun not only to question but, having arrived at answers, to act on those answers. This is a part of a growing understanding among many people in America that history has not ended, that a better society is possible, and that it is worth dying for.

This free-speech fight points up a fascinating aspect of contemporary campus life. Students are permitted to talk all they want so long as their speech has no consequences. . . . Someone may advocate radical change in all aspects of American society, and this I am sure he can do with impunity. But if someone advocates sit-ins to bring about changes in discriminatory hiring practices, this cannot be permitted because it goes against the status quo of which the university is a part. . . .

The most exciting things going on in America today are movements to change America. America is becoming ever more the utopia of sterilized, automated contentment. The "futures" and "careers" for which American students now prepare are for the most part intellectual and moral wastelands. This chrome-plated consumers' paradise would have us grow up to be well-behaved children. But an important minority of men and women coming to the front today have shown that they will die rather than be standardized, replaceable and irrelevant.

☆

Lyndon Baines Johnson

"We Shall Overcome"

Congress, Washington, D.C.
March 15, 1965

Vice president Lyndon Baines Johnson became president when John F. Kennedy was assassinated in 1963. As a southerner from Texas, Johnson felt a special responsibility for improving civil rights for all Americans. When civil rights marchers in Selma, Alabama, were beaten by police on a "Bloody Sunday" that shocked America, just days later Johnson called on Congress to pass his Voting Rights Act to ensure for black Americans the right to vote. Writing up until the last moment, he delivered the finest speech of his presidency and in an inspired moment declared, "We shall overcome," a quote from the civil rights hymn.

☆ ☆

I speak tonight for the dignity of man and the destiny of democracy.

I urge every member of both parties, Americans of all religions and of all colors, from every section of this country, to join me in that cause.

At times history and fate meet at a single time in a single place to shape a turning point in man's unending search for freedom. So it was at Lexington and Concord. So it was a century ago at Appomattox. So it was last week in Selma, Alabama. There, long-suffering men and women peacefully protested the denial of their rights as Americans. Many were brutally assaulted. One good man, a man of God, was killed. . . .

In our time we have come to live with moments of great crisis. Our lives have been marked with debate about great issues; issues of war and peace, issues of prosperity and depression. But rarely in any time does an issue lay bare the secret heart of America itself. Rarely are we met with a challenge, not to our growth or abundance, our welfare or our security; but rather to the values and the purposes and the meaning of our beloved nation.

The issue of equal rights for American Negroes is such an issue. And should we defeat every enemy, should we double our wealth and conquer the stars, and still be unequal to this issue, then we will have failed as a people and as a nation. For with a country as with a person, "What is a man profited, if he shall gain the whole world, and lose his own soul?"

There is no Negro problem. There is no Southern problem. There is no Northern problem. There is only an American problem. And we are met here tonight as Americans—not as Democrats or Republicans—we are met here as Americans to solve that problem.

This was the first nation in the history of the world to be founded with a purpose. The great phrases of that purpose still sound in every American heart, North and South: "All men are created equal"; "government by consent of the governed"; "give me liberty or give me death." . . . To deny a man his hopes because of his color or race, his religion or the place of his birth—is not only to do injustice, it is to deny America and to dishonor the dead who gave their lives for American freedom.

Our fathers believed that if this noble view of the rights of man was to flourish, it must be rooted in democracy. The most basic right of all was the right to choose your own leaders. . . .

Yet the harsh fact is that in many places in this country men and women are kept from voting simply because they are Negroes. Every device of which human ingenuity is capable has been used to deny this right. The Negro citizen may go to register only to be told that the day is wrong, or the hour is late, or the official in charge is absent. . . . He may be asked to recite the entire Constitution, or explain the most complex provisions of state law. And even a college degree cannot be used to prove that he can read and write. For the fact is that the only way to pass these barriers is to show a white skin.

Wednesday, I will send to Congress a law designed to elim-inate illegal barriers to the right to vote. . . . But even if we pass this bill, the battle will not be over. What happened in Selma is part of a far larger movement which reaches into every section and state of America. It is the effort of American Negroes to secure for themselves the full blessings of Ameri-can life.

Their cause must be our cause too. Because it is not just Negroes, but really it is all of us, who must overcome the crip-pling legacy of bigotry and injustice.

And we shall overcome. . . .

A century has passed, more than a hundred years, since equality was promised. And yet the Negro is not equal. A cen-tury has passed since the day of promise. And the promise is unkept.

The time of justice has now come. I tell you that I believe sincerely that no force can hold it back. It is right in the eyes of man and God that it should come. And when it does, I think that day will brighten the lives of every American. For Negroes are not the only victims. How many white children have gone uneducated, how many white families have lived in stark poverty, how many white lives have been scarred by fear, because we have wasted our energy and our substance to maintain the barriers of hatred and terror? . . .

My first job after college was as a teacher in Cotulla, Texas, in a small Mexican-American school. Few of them could speak English, and I couldn't speak much Spanish. My stu-dents were poor and they often came to class without break-fast, hungry. They knew even in their youth the pain of prejudice. They never seemed to know why people disliked them. But they knew it was so, because I saw it in their eyes. I often walked home late in the afternoon, after the classes were finished, wishing there was more that I could do. But all I knew was to teach them the little that I knew, hoping that it might help them against the hardships that lay ahead.

Somehow you never forget what poverty and hatred can do

when you see its scars on the hopeful face of a young child. I never thought then, in 1928, that I would be standing here in 1965. It never even occurred to me in my fondest dreams that I might have the chance to help the sons and daughters of those students and to help people like them all over this country. But now I do have that chance. . . .

I want to be the president who helped the poor to find their own way and who protected the right of every citizen to vote in every election. I want to be the president who helped to end hatred among his fellow men and who promoted love among the people of all races and all regions and all parties. I want to be the president who helped to end war among the brothers of this earth.

And so . . . I came down here to ask you to share this task with me and to share it with the people that we both work for. I want this to be the Congress, Republicans and Democrats alike, which did all these things for all these people.

☆

Adlai Stevenson

To the United Nations

Geneva, Switzerland
July 9, 1965

Adlai Stevenson served a term as governor of Illinois and twice ran unsuccessfully for the presidency against Dwight D. Eisenhower. He worked for the United Nations in its early years after World War II, and in 1961 President Kennedy returned him as U.S. ambassador to the United Nations. His last speech, to the U.N. Economic and Social Council, was in keeping with his lifelong interest in reform and the furthering of a peaceful world community.

☆ ☆

We meet here in Geneva at the midpoint of the Year of International Cooperation and the midpoint of the Decade of Development. Let us be neither cynical nor despondent about the gap between these brave titles and the fact that at the moment, our world community is in fact chiefly notable for minimal cooperation and very lopsided development. Our aspirations are there to spur us on, to incite us to better efforts. . . .

Let's face it: We are nowhere near conquering world poverty. None of us—neither the weak nor the strong, the poor nor the rich, the new nations nor the old—have yet taken seriously enough the contrast between the abundance of our opportunities and the scarcity of our actions to grasp them. It is good that the rich are getting richer—that is what economic development is for. But it is bad that despite our considerable efforts in the first half of this decade, the poor are still poor—and progressing more slowly than present-day society can tolerate. What shall we do to improve the trend during the next five years? There is something for everybody to do. . . .

Joint action is, after all, the final significance of all we do in our international policies today. But we are still held back by our old parochial nationalisms. We are still beset with dark prejudices. We are still divided by angry, conflicting ideologies. Yet all around us our science, our instruments, our technologies, our interests and indeed our deepest aspirations draw us more and more closely into a single neighborhood.

This must be the context of our thinking—the context of human interdependence in the face of the vast new dimensions of our science and our discovery. Just as Europe could never again be the old, closed-in community after the voyages of Columbus, we can never again be a squabbling band of nations before the awful majesty of outer space.

We travel together, passengers on a little space ship, dependent on its vulnerable reserves of air and soil; all committed for our safety to its security and peace; preserved from annihilation only by the care, the work, and, I will say, the love we give our fragile craft. We cannot maintain it half fortunate, half miserable, half confident, half despairing, half slave—to the ancient enemies of man—half free in a liberation of resources undreamed of until this day. No craft, no crew can travel safely with such vast contradictions. On their resolution depends the survival of us all.

☆

William Sloane Coffin Jr.

"The Anvil of Individual Conscience"

Washington, D.C.
October 20, 1967

In the early 1960s, the United States joined South Vietnam in a war against North Vietnam in an attempt to prevent the spread of that nation's communism. At home, the Vietnam War became extremely unpopular, and students, professors, and increasingly the clergy moved to the forefront in opposing the war. Yale Chaplain William Sloane Coffin Jr., who had been jailed repeatedly in the South for protesting segregation, joined the movement against the military draft. In 1967, he addressed a crowd at the Justice Department in Washington as hundreds of draft cards from across the United States were turned in to protest the war. He was later arrested for aiding draft evasion.

☆ ☆

What we are here to do is not a natural, easy thing for any of us. We are writers, professors, clergy, and this is not our "thing." But we have come here to be with conscientious men in their hour of conscience; and because like them we cannot stand around with dry feet while wisdom and decency go under for the third time in Vietnam.

This week once again high government officials described protesters against the war as "naive," "wild-eyed idealists." But in our view it is not wild-eyed idealism but clear-eyed revulsion that brings us here. For as one of our number put it: "If what the United States is doing in Vietnam is right, what is there left to be called wrong?"

Many of us are veterans, and all of us have the highest sympathy for our boys in Vietnam. They know what a dirty, bloody war it is. But they have been told that the ends justify the means, and that the cleansing water of victory will wash clean their hands of all the blood and dirt. . . . But what they

231

must strive to understand, hard as it is, is that there can be no cleansing water if military victory spells moral defeat.

We have the highest sympathy also for those who back the war because their sons or lovers or husbands are fighting or have died in Vietnam. But they too must understand a very basic thing—that sacrifice in and of itself confers no sanctity. Even if half a million of our boys were to die in Vietnam that would not make the cause one whit more sacred. Yet we realize how hard that knowledge is to appropriate when one's husband is numbered among the sacrificed.

The mother of a son lost in Vietnam once told me "My son used to write how much he and his company were doing for the orphans. But I used to answer 'If you want to help the orphans, son, you must stop killing their fathers and mothers.'"

Like this mother we do not dispute the good intentions, the good works of endless good Americans in Vietnam. But we do insist that no amount of good intentions nor good works, nor certainly government rhetoric to the contrary, can offset the fact that American policy in Vietnam . . . has run amok. The war is not only unwise but unjust, and if that is true then it is not we who are demoralizing our boys in Vietnam, but the government, which asks them to do immoral things.

As the war to us is immoral, so also is the draft. For the National Selective Service Act not only places the major burden of the war on the backs of the poor; it also confronts thousands of men with a choice of either violating their consciences or going to jail. . . .

We admire the way these young men who could safely have hidden behind exemptions and deferments have elected instead to risk something big for something good. We admire them and believe theirs is the true voice of America, the vision that will prevail beyond the distortions of the moment.

We cannot shield them. We can only expose ourselves as they have done. The law of the land is clear. Section 12 of the National Selective Service Act declares that anyone "who knowingly counsels, aids, or abets another to refuse or evade registration or service in the armed forces . . . shall be liable to imprisonment for not more than five years or a fine of ten thousand dollars or both."

We hereby publicly counsel these young men to continue in their refusal to serve in the armed forces as long as the war in Vietnam continues, and we pledge ourselves to aid and abet them in all the ways we can. This means that if they are now arrested for failing to comply with a law that violates their consciences, we too must be arrested, for in the sight of that law we are now as guilty as they.

It is a long-standing tradition, sanctioned by American democracy, that the dictates of government must be tested on the anvil of individual conscience. This is what we now undertake to do—not as a first but as a last resort. And in accepting the legal punishment we are, in fact, supporting, not subverting, the legal order.

Still, to stand in this fashion against the law and before our fellow Americans is a difficult and even fearful thing. But in the face of what to us is insane and inhuman we can fall neither silent nor servile. Nor can we educate young men to be conscientious only to desert them in their hour of conscience. So we are resolved, as they are resolved, to speak out clearly and to pay up personally.

Cesar Chavez addresses a rally for the United Farm Workers.

Cesar Chavez

"God Help Us to Be Men!"

Delano, California
March 10, 1968

Cesar Chavez lived the harsh life of a California migrant farm worker as a Mexican American child. Later he founded the United Farm Workers, a union committed to nonviolent action for higher wages and better working conditions for impoverished farm workers. Chavez periodically fasted to draw attention to their plight, and at the end of his first twenty-five-day fast, he had a message for the eight thousand people gathered to celebrate.

☆ ☆

I have asked the Reverend James Drake to read this statement to you because my heart is so full and my body too weak to be able to say what I feel.

My warm thanks to all of you for coming today. Many of you have been here before, during the fast. Some have sent beautiful cards and telegrams and made offerings at the Mass. All of these expressions of your love have strengthened me and I am grateful.

234

We should all express our thanks to Senator Kennedy for his constant work on behalf of the poor, for his personal encouragement to me, and for taking the time to break bread with us today. . . .

We are gathered here today not so much to observe the end of the fast but because we are a family bound together in a common struggle for justice. We are a union family celebrating our unity and the nonviolent nature of our movement. Perhaps in the future we will come together at other times and places to break bread and to renew our courage and to celebrate important victories.

The fast has had different meanings for different people. Some of you may still wonder about its meaning and importance. It was not intended as a pressure against any growers. For that reason we have suspended negotiations and arbitration proceedings and relaxed the militant picketing and boycotting of the strike during this period. I undertook this fast because my heart was filled with grief and pain for the sufferings of farm workers. The fast was first for me and then for all of us in this union. It was a fast for nonviolence and a call to sacrifice.

Our struggle is not easy. Those who oppose our cause are rich and powerful and they have many allies in high places. We are poor. Our allies are few. But we have something the rich do not own. We have our own bodies and spirits and the justice of our cause as our weapons.

When we are really honest with ourselves we must admit that our lives are all that really belong to us. So, it is how we use our lives that determines what kind of men we are. It is my deepest belief that only by giving our lives do we find life. I am convinced that the truest act of courage, the strongest act of manliness is to sacrifice ourselves for others in a totally nonviolent struggle for justice. To be a man is to suffer for others. God help us to be men!

☆

J. William Fulbright

"The Focus Is Vietnam"

Washington, D.C.
March 11, 1968

William Fulbright was president of the University of Arkansas when he was 34, and went on to serve in the U.S. Senate for thirty years and foster the Fulbright Scholarship program to exchange American and foreign students. In 1968, as a senator from Arkansas and chairman of the Senate Foreign Relations Committee, he opened hearings (with Secretary of State Dean Rusk) on the Vietnam War. Requests by the military for 200,000 more troops had awakened fears of a serious escalation of the war, leading many more people to question American involvement in Vietnam.

☆ ☆

It goes without saying, or should go without saying, that our disagreements have nothing to do with whether one is for or against America. We are all for America and for America's interests. But we disagree as to what those interests are and how they can best be advanced.

We are all for America's prosperity at home and for its prestige abroad, but we disagree as to which requires precedence in these critical days. We are all for our fighting men in Vietnam, but we disagree as to whether they ought to be fighting there, as to whether the cause to which we have submitted them is worth their lives and their terrible sacrifices.

These are not trivial disagreements and it would be a disservice to the country to pretend that they are insignificant.

The focus is Vietnam and where the issue has become very much more than the fate of a poor, small and war-torn Asian nation, the question is also the fate of America not because it had to be so but because our leaders have made it so.

By committing half a million of our young men to bloody

and endless combat in these distant jungles our leaders have converted a struggle between Vietnamese for possession of the Vietnamese land into a struggle between Americans for possession of the American spirit. . . .

There was a time not so long ago when Americans believed that whatever else they might have to do in the world, whatever wars they might have to fight, whatever aid they might have to provide, their principal contribution to the world would be their own example as a decent and democratic society. Now, with our country beset by crises of poverty and race as we wait and arm ourselves for the annual summer of violence in our cities, with our allies alienated and our people divided by the most unpopular war in our history, the light of the American example burns dim around the world. More alarming still is the dimming of the light of optimism among the American people, especially among our youths who . . . having believed too well what they were brought up to believe in, have arisen in a kind of spiritual rebellion against what they regard as the betrayal of a traditional American value.

The signs of the rebellion are all around us, not just in the hippie movement and in the emergence of an angry New Left, but in the sharp decline of applications for the Peace Corps, in the turning away of promising students from careers in government, in letters of protest against the war and troubled consciences about the draft.

It is sometimes said that [with] our huge national product, we can easily afford the 30 billion dollars a year we're spending on the war in Vietnam.

Perhaps in purely financial terms we can afford it, although I for one am far from convinced. But even if we can afford the money, can we afford the sacrifice of American lives in so dubious a cause? Can we afford the horrors which are being inflicted on the people of a poor and backward land to say nothing of our own people? Can we afford the alienation of our allies, the neglect of our own deep domestic problems and the disillusionment of our youth? Can we afford the loss of confidence in our government and institutions, the fading of hope and optimism and the betrayal of our traditional values?

These, Mr. Secretary, are some of the questions that have to be put before we can return, or I can return, to the normal legislative activities which technically are before the committee today.

☆

Martin Luther King Jr.

"I've Been to the Mountaintop"

Memphis, Tennessee
April 3, 1968

In Memphis to support striking sanitation workers, Martin Luther King Jr. appeared to foresee his own death in this last sermon given at Mason Temple the day before he was assassinated.

☆ ☆

I want to thank God, once more, for allowing me to be here with you.

You know, several years ago, I was in New York City autographing the first book that I had written. And while sitting there autographing books, a demented black woman came up. The only question I heard from her was, "Are you Martin Luther King?"

And I was looking down writing, and I said yes. And the next minute I felt something beating on my chest. Before I knew it I had been stabbed by this demented woman. I was rushed to Harlem Hospital. It was a dark Saturday afternoon. And that blade had gone through, and the X-rays revealed that the tip of the blade was on the edge of my aorta, the main artery. And once that's punctured, you drown in your own blood—that's the end of you.

It came out in the *New York Times* the next morning, that if I had sneezed, I would have died. Well, about four days later, they allowed me, after the operation, after my chest had been opened, and the blade had been taken out, to move around in the wheelchair in the hospital. They allowed me to read some of the mail that came in, and from all over the states, and the world, kind letters came in. I read a few, but one of them I will never forget. I had received one from the President and Vice

239

President. I've forgotten what those telegrams said. I'd received a visit and a letter from the Governor of New York, but I've forgotten what the letter said. But there was another letter that came from a little girl, a young girl who was a student at the White Plains High School. And I looked at that letter, and I'll never forget it. It said simply, "Dear Dr. King: I am a ninth-grade student at the White Plains High School." She said, "While it should not matter, I would like to mention that I am a white girl. I read in the paper of your misfortune, and of your suffering. And I read that if you had sneezed, you would have died. And I'm simply writing you to say that I'm so happy that you didn't sneeze."

And I want to say tonight, I want to say that I am happy that I didn't sneeze. Because if I had sneezed, I wouldn't have been around here in 1960, when students all over the South started sitting-in at lunch counters. And I knew that as they were sitting in, they were really standing up for the best in the American dream. And taking the whole nation back to those great wells of democracy which were dug deep by the Founding Fathers in the Declaration of Independence and the Constitution.

If I had sneezed, I wouldn't have been around in 1962, when Negroes in Albany, Georgia, decided to straighten their backs up. And whenever men and women straighten their backs up, they are going somewhere, because a man can't ride your back unless it is bent.

If I had sneezed, I wouldn't have been here in 1963, when the black people of Birmingham, Alabama, aroused the conscience of this nation, and brought into being the Civil Rights Bill. If I had sneezed, I wouldn't have had a chance later that year, in August, to try to tell Americans about a dream that I had had. If I had sneezed, I wouldn't have been down in Selma, Alabama, to see the great movement there. If I had sneezed, I wouldn't have been in Memphis to see a community rally around those brothers and sisters who are suffering. I'm so happy that I didn't sneeze. . . .

I left Atlanta this morning, and as we got started on the

plane, there were six of us, the pilot said over the public address system, "We are sorry for the delay, but we have Dr. Martin Luther King on the plane. And to be sure that all of the bags were checked, and to be sure that nothing would be wrong with the plane, we had to check out everything carefully. And we've had the plane protected and guarded all night."

And then I got into Memphis. And some began to say the threats, or talk about the threats that were out. What would happen to me from some of our sick white brothers?

Well, I don't know what will happen now. We've got some difficult days ahead. But it doesn't matter with me now. Because I've been to the mountaintop. And I don't mind. Like anybody, I would like to live a long life. Longevity has its place. But I'm not concerned about that now. I just want to do God's will. And He's allowed me to go up to the mountain. And I've looked over. And I've seen the promised land. I may not get there with you. But I want you to know tonight, that we, as a people will get to the promised land. And I'm happy, tonight. I'm not worried about anything. I'm not fearing any man. Mine eyes have seen the glory of the coming of the Lord.

Robert F. Kennedy surveys the damage from rioting in Washington, D.C.,
after the death of Martin Luther King Jr.

Robert F. Kennedy

On the Assassination of Martin Luther King Jr.

Indianapolis, Indiana
April 4, 1968

Robert F. Kennedy, John F. Kennedy's brother and a senator from Massachusetts,
was already scheduled to speak to a black audience in Indianapolis on the evening
of the day Martin Luther King was assassinated. He had the difficult task of
breaking the news of the tragedy to the unprepared listeners, and, putting aside his
prepared speech, he appealed for love and compassion in place of violence. Shortly
after, rioting broke out in over a hundred American cities with dozens of deaths,
but Indianapolis stayed calm. Kennedy was himself assassinated while campaign-
ing for president two months later.

☆ ☆

I have bad news for you, for all of our fellow citizens, and people who love peace all over the world, and that is that Martin Luther King was shot and killed tonight.

Martin Luther King dedicated his life to love and to justice for his fellow human beings, and he died because of that effort.

In this difficult day, in this difficult time for the United States, it is perhaps well to ask what kind of a nation we are and what direction we want to move in. For those of you who are black—considering the evidence there evidently is that there were white people who were responsible—you can be filled with bitterness, with hatred, and a desire for revenge. We can move in that direction as a country, in great polarization—black people amongst black, white people amongst white, filled with hatred toward one another.

Or we can make an effort, as Martin Luther King did, to understand and to comprehend, and to replace that violence, that stain of bloodshed that has spread across our land, with an effort to understand with compassion and love.

For those of you who are black and are tempted to be filled with hatred and distrust at the injustice of such an act, against all white people, I can only say that I feel in my own heart the same kind of feeling. I had a member of my family killed, but he was killed by a white man. But we have to make an effort in the United States, we have to make an effort to understand, to go beyond these rather difficult times.

My favorite poet was Aeschylus. He wrote, "In our sleep, pain which cannot forget falls drop by drop upon the heart until, in our own despair, against our will, comes wisdom through the awful grace of God."

What we need in the United States is not division; what we need in the United States is not hatred; what we need in the United States is not violence or lawlessness but love and wisdom, and compassion toward one another, and a feeling of justice towards those who still suffer within our country, whether they be white or whether they be black.

So I shall ask you tonight to return home, to say a prayer for the family of Martin Luther King, that's true, but more importantly to say a prayer for our own country, which all of us love—a prayer for understanding and that compassion of which I spoke.

We can do well in this country. We will have difficult times. We've had difficult times in the past. We will have difficult times in the future. It is not the end of violence; it is not the end of lawlessness; it is not the end of disorder.

But the vast majority of white people and the vast majority of black people in this country want to live together, want to improve the quality of our life, and want justice for all human beings who abide in our land.

Let us dedicate ourselves to what the Greeks wrote so many years ago: to tame the savageness of man and to make gentle the life of this world.

Let us dedicate ourselves to that, and say a prayer for our country and for our people.

☆

Shirley Chisholm

"The Business of America Is War"

U.S. House of Representatives, Washington, D.C.
March 26, 1969

Shirley Chisholm of Brooklyn, New York, was a teacher for over twenty years
before she entered politics. She held office in the New York State Assembly, then
became the first black woman elected to the U.S. Congress. In March of 1969, she
made her first speech to the House of Representatives, lamenting the expense of the
Vietnam War and the neglect of social issues at home in the United States.

☆ ☆

Mr. Speaker, on the same day President Nixon announced
he had decided the United States will not be safe unless
we start to build a defense system against missiles, the Head-
start program in the District of Columbia was cut back for the
lack of money.

As a teacher, and as a woman, I do not think I will ever
understand what kind of values can be involved in spending
nine billion dollars—and more, I am sure—on elaborate,
unnecessary and impractical weapons when several thousand
disadvantaged children in the nation's capital get nothing.

When the new administration took office, I was one of the
many Americans who hoped it would mean that our country
would benefit from the fresh perspectives, the new ideas, the
different priorities of a leader who had no part in the mistakes
of the past. Mr. Nixon had said things like this:

"If our cities are to be livable for the next generation, we
can delay no longer in launching new approaches to the problems that beset them and to the tensions that tear them
apart."

And he said, "When you cut expenditures for education,
what you are doing is shortchanging the American future."

But frankly, I have never cared too much what people say. What I am interested in is what they do. We have waited to see what the new administration is going to do. The pattern now is becoming clear.

Apparently launching those new programs can be delayed for a while, after all. It seems we have to get some missiles launched first. . . .

Secretary of Defense Melvin Laird came to Capitol Hill. . . . Mr. Laird talked of being prepared to spend at least two more years in Vietnam.

Two more years, two more years of hunger for Americans, of death for our best young men, of children here at home suffering the lifelong handicap of not having a good education when they are young. Two more years of high taxes, collected to feed the cancerous growth of a Defense Department budget that now consumes two thirds of our federal income. . . .

We Americans have come to feel that it is our mission to make the world free. We believe that we are the good guys, everywhere—in Vietnam, in Latin America, wherever we go. We believe we are the good guys at home, too. When the Kerner Commission told white America what black America had always known, that prejudice and hatred built the nation's slums, maintain them and profit by them, white America would not believe it. But it is true. Unless we start to fight and defeat the enemies of poverty and racism in our own country and make our talk of equality and opportunity ring true, we are exposed as hypocrites in the eyes of the world when we talk about making other people free.

I am deeply disappointed at the clear evidence that the number-one priority of the new administration is to buy more and more weapons of war, to return to the era of the cold war, to ignore the war we must fight here—the war that is not optional. . . .

For this reason, I intend to vote "No" on every money bill that comes to the floor of this House that provides any funds for the Department of Defense. Any bill whatsoever, until the time comes when our values and priorities have been turned right side up again, until the monstrous waste and the shocking profits in the defense budget have been eliminated and our country starts to use its strength, its tremendous resources, for people and peace, not for profits and war.

It was Calvin Coolidge, I believe, who made the comment that "the Business of America is Business." We are now spending eighty billion dollars a year on defense—that is two thirds of every tax dollar. At this time, gentlemen, the business of America is war, and it is time for a change.

☆

Frank James

On the 350th Anniversary of Plymouth

Boston, Massachusetts
September 11, 1970

Frank James was a descendant of the Wampanoags, the Native American people the Pilgrims first encountered in 1620 on their arrival in the New World. He was invited to speak at the governor's banquet celebrating the 350th anniversary of the Pilgrims' landing at Plymouth, Massachusetts, an honor performed by the great orator Daniel Webster at the 200th anniversary in 1820. When the organizers read James's speech beforehand, however, he was not permitted to deliver it. Angered by this censorship, over 500 Indians protested at Plymouth Rock that Thanksgiving, and a Day of Mourning has been held every year since.

☆☆

It is with mixed emotions that I stand here to share my thoughts. This is a time of celebration for you—celebrating an anniversary of a beginning for the white man in America. A time of looking back—of reflection. It is with heavy heart that I look back upon what happened to my People.

Even before the Pilgrims landed it was common practice for explorers to capture Indians, take them to Europe and sell them as slaves for 220 shillings apiece. The Pilgrims had hardly explored the shores of Cape Cod four days before they had robbed the graves of my ancestors, and stolen their corn, wheat, and beans. . . .

Massasoit, the great Sachem of the Wampanoag knew these facts, yet he and his People welcomed and befriended the settlers of the Plymouth Plantation. . . . This action by Massasoit was probably our greatest mistake. We, the Wampanoags, welcomed you, the white man with open arms, little knowing that it was the beginning of the end; that before 50 years were to pass, the Wampanoags would no longer be a Tribe. . . .

248

High on a hill, overlooking the famed Plymouth Rock stands the statue of our great Sachem, Massasoit. Massasoit has stood there many years in silence. We the descendants of this great sachem have been a silent People. The necessity of making a living in this materialistic society of the white man caused us to be silent. Today, I and many of my People are choosing to face the truth. We ARE Indians!

Although time has drained our culture, and our language is almost extinct, we the Wampanoags still walk the lands of Massachusetts. We may be fragmented, we may be confused. Many years have passed since we have been a People together. Our lands were invaded. We fought as hard to keep our land as you the white did to take our land away from us. We were conquered, we became the American Prisoners of War in many cases, and wards of the United States Government until only recently.

Our spirit refuses to die. Yesterday we walked the woodland paths and sandy trails. Today we must walk the macadam highways and roads. We are uniting. We're standing not in our wigwams but in your concrete tent. We stand tall and proud and before too many moons pass we'll right the wrongs we have allowed to happen to us.

We forfeited our country. Our lands have fallen into the hands of the aggressor. We have allowed the white man to keep us on our knees. What has happened cannot be changed but today we work towards a more humane America, a more Indian America where men and nature once again are important; where the Indian values of honor, truth and brotherhood prevail.

You the white man are celebrating an anniversary. We the Wampanoags will help you celebrate in the concept of a beginning. It was the beginning of a new life for the Pilgrims. Now, 350 years later it is a beginning of a new determination for the original American—The American Indian.

We now have 350 years of experience living amongst the white man. We can now speak his language. We can now think as a white man thinks. We can now compete with him for the top jobs. We're being heard; we are now being listened to. The important point is that along with these necessities of everyday living, we still have the spirit, we still have a unique culture, we still have the will and most important of all, the determination to remain as Indians.

We are determined, and our presence here this evening is living testimony that this is only a beginning of the American Indian, particularly the Wampanoag, to regain the position in this country that is rightfully ours.

Archibald Cox

"The Price of Liberty to Speak the Truth"

Cambridge, Massachusetts
March 26, 1971

Later to serve as special prosecutor investigating President Nixon's Watergate scandal, Archibald Cox was professor of law at Harvard University. During the Vietnam War, he bravely defended the rights of pro-war South Vietnamese and United States spokesmen to address a university audience, all the while being pelted with debris and drowned out by the shouting of a thousand antiwar protestors, until he and the invited speakers abandoned the stage and escaped through the steam tunnels beneath the building.

☆ ☆

My name is Archibald Cox. I beseech you to let me say a few words in the name of the President and Fellows of this university on behalf of freedom of speech. For if this meeting is disrupted—hateful as some of us may find it—then liberty will have died a little and those guilty of the disruption will have done inestimable damage to the causes of humanity and peace.

Men and women whose views aroused strong emotions— loved by some and hated by others—have always been allowed to speak at Harvard—Fidel Castro, the late Malcolm X, George Wallace, William Kuntsler, and others. Last year, in this very building, speeches were made for physical obstruction of university activities. Harvard gave a platform to all these speakers, even those calling for her destruction. No one in the community tried to silence them, despite intense opposition.

The reason is plain, and it applies here tonight. Freedom of speech is indivisible. You cannot deny it to one man and save it for others. Over and over again the test of our dedication to liberty is our willingness to allow the expression of ideas we hate. If those ideas are lies, the remedy is more speech and more debate, so that men will learn the truth—speech like the teach-in here a few weeks ago. To clap down or shout down a speaker on the ground that his ideas are dangerous or that he is telling a lie is to license all others to silence the speakers and suppress the publications with which they disagree. Suppose that speech is suppressed here tonight. Have you confidence that all who follow the example will be as morally right as they suppose themselves to be? History is filled with examples of the cruelty inflicted by men who set out to suppress ideas in the conviction of their own moral righteousness. This time those who have talked of disruption have a moral purpose, and may indeed be right in their goals and objectives. But will others be equally right when they resort to the same tactics? The price of liberty to speak the truth as each of us sees it is permitting others the same freedom.

Disruptive tactics seem to say, "We are scared to let others speak for fear that the listeners will believe them and not us." Disruptive tactics, even by noise alone, start us on the road to more and more disruption, and then to violence and more violence, because each group will come prepared the next time with greater numbers and ready to use a little more force until in the end, as in Hitler's Germany, all that counts is brute power.

And so I cling to the hope that those of you who started to prevent the speakers from being heard will desist. You have the power to disrupt the meeting, I am quite sure. The disciplinary action that will surely follow is not likely to deter you. But I hope that your good sense and courage in doing what's right will cause you to change your minds—to refrain from doing grievous and perhaps irretrievable harm to liberty.

Answer what is said here with more teach-ins and more truth, but let the speakers be heard.

Barbara Jordan

"My Faith in the Constitution Is Whole"

U.S. House of Representatives, Washington, D.C.
July 25, 1974

Barbara Jordan was a leading debater on her winning high school team in Houston, Texas. Later she became the first black woman from the South ever elected to Congress. As a member of the House Judiciary Committee, she delivered a brilliant opening statement during the televised proceedings on the impeachment of President Richard Nixon. Her careful explanation of the Constitution and the charges against the president made her known to the nation.

☆ ☆

Mr. Chairman, . . . Earlier today we heard the beginning of the Preamble to the Constitution of the United States, "We, the people." It is a very eloquent beginning. But when that document was completed on the seventeenth of September in 1787 I was not included in that "We, the people." I felt somehow for many years that George Washington and Alexander Hamilton just left me out by mistake. But through the process of amendment, interpretation and court decision I have finally been included in "We, the people."

Today, I am an inquisitor. I . . . would not overstate the solemnness that I feel right now. My faith in the Constitution is whole, it is complete, it is total. I am not going to sit here and be an idle spectator to the diminuition, the subversion, the destruction of the Constitution.

"Who can so properly be the inquisitors for the nation as the representatives of the nation themselves? The subject of its jurisdiction are those offenses which proceed from the misconduct of public men" [*Federalist Papers*, number 65]. That is what we are talking about. In other words, the jurisdiction comes from the abuse or violation of some public trust. . . .

253

The powers relating to impeachment are an essential check in the hands of this body, the legislature, against and upon the encroachment of the executive. In establishing the division between the two branches of the legislature, the House and the Senate, assigning to the one the right to accuse and to the other the right to judge, the Framers of this Constitution were very astute. They did not make the accusers and the judges the same person.

We know the nature of impeachment. We have been talking about it awhile now. "It is chiefly designed for the president and his high ministers" to somehow be called into account. It is designed to "bridle" the executive if he engages in excesses. "It is designed as a method of national inquest into the conduct of public men." The Framers confined in the Congress the power, if need be, to remove the president in order to strike a delicate balance between a president swollen with power and grown tyrannical, and preservation of the independence of the executive. . . . "It is to be used only for great misdemeanors," so it was said in the North Carolina ratification convention. . . .

Common sense would be revolted if we engaged upon this process for petty reasons. Congress has a lot to do. Appropriations, tax reform, health insurance, campaign finance reform, housing, environmental protection, energy sufficiency, mass transportation. Pettiness cannot be allowed to stand in the face of such overwhelming problems. So today we are not being petty. We are trying to be big because the task we have before us is a big one. . . .

At this point I would like to juxtapose a few of the impeachment criteria with some of the president's actions.

Impeachment criteria: James Madison, from the Virginia ratification convention, "If the president be connected in any suspicious manner with any person and there be grounds to believe that he will shelter him, he may be impeached."

We have heard time and time again that the evidence reflects payment to the defendants of money. The president had knowledge that these funds were being paid and that these were funds collected for the 1972 presidential campaign. . . .

The South Carolina ratification convention impeachment criteria: Those are impeachable "who behave amiss or betray their public trust."

Beginning shortly after the Watergate break-in and continuing to the present time the president has engaged in a series of public statements and actions designed to thwart the lawful investigation by government prosecutors. Moreover, the president has made public announcements and assertions bearing on the Watergate case which the evidence will show he knew to be false. . . .

James Madison again at the constitutional convention: "A president is impeachable if he attempts to subvert the Constitution."

The Constitution charges the president with the task of taking care that the laws be faithfully executed, and yet the president has counseled his aides to commit perjury, willfully disregarded the secrecy of grand jury proceedings, concealed surreptitious entry, attempted to compromise a federal judge while publicly displaying his cooperation with the processes of criminal justice. "A president is impeachable if he attempts to subvert the Constitution."

If the impeachment provision in the Constitution of the United States will not reach the offenses charged here, then perhaps that eighteenth century Constitution should be abandoned to a twentieth century paper shredder. Has the president committed offenses and planned and directed and acquiesced in a course of conduct which the Constitution will not tolerate? That is the question. We know that. We know the question. We should now forthwith proceed to answer the question. It is reason, and not passion, which must guide our deliberations, guide our debate, and guide our decision.

☆

Richard Nixon

"I Shall Resign the Presidency"

Washington, D.C.
August 8, 1974

Richard Nixon won a second term as president with a landslide election in November of 1972. But a subsequent investigation of a break-in at the campaign headquarters of the Democratic Party in the Watergate office building in Washington revealed a conspiracy that implicated the president and his aides. After the House Judiciary Committee voted to impeach the president for his part in the cover-up, Nixon decided to resign from office.

☆ ☆

Throughout the long and difficult period of Watergate, I have felt it was my duty to persevere, to make every possible effort to complete the term of office to which you elected me. In the past few days, however, it has become evident to me that I no longer have a strong enough political base in the Congress to justify continuing that effort. . . .

Therefore, I shall resign the presidency effective at noon tomorrow. Vice President Ford will be sworn in as president at that hour in this office. . . .

I regret deeply any injuries that may have been done in the course of the events that led to this decision. I would say only that if some of my judgments were wrong—and some were wrong—they were made in what I believed at the time to be the best interests of the nation. . . .

Let me say I leave with no bitterness toward those who have opposed me, because all of us in the final analysis have been concerned with the good of the country, however our judgments might differ. So let us all now join together in affirming that common commitment and in helping our new president succeed for the benefit of all Americans.

We have ended America's longest war. But in the work of securing a lasting peace in the world, the goals ahead are even more far-reaching and more difficult. We must complete a structure of peace, so that it will be said of this generation— our generation of Americans—by the people of all nations, not only that we ended one war but that we prevented future wars. . . .

For more than a quarter of a century in public life, I have shared in the turbulent history of this evening.

I have fought for what I believe in. I have tried, to the best of my ability, to discharge those duties and meet those responsibilities that were entrusted to me.

Sometimes I have succeeded. And sometimes I have failed. But always I have taken heart from what Theodore Roosevelt said about the man in the arena whose face is marred by dust and sweat and blood, who strives valiantly, who errs and comes short again and again because there is not effort without error and shortcoming, but who does actually strive to do the deed, who knows the great devotion, who spends himself in a worthy cause, who at the best knows in the end the triumphs of high achievements and with the worst if he fails, at least fails while daring greatly.

I pledge to you tonight that as long as I have a breath of life in my body I shall continue in that spirit. I shall continue to work for the great causes to which I have been dedicated throughout my years as a congressman, a senator, vice president, and president, the cause of peace—not just for America but among all nations—prosperity, justice, and opportunity for all our people. . . .

As a result of these efforts, I am confident that the world is a safer place today, not only for the people of America but for the people of all nations, and that all of our children have a better chance than before of living in peace rather than dying in war.

Silvio Conte

"I Must 'Raise a Beef' about This Bill"

U.S. House of Representatives, Washington, D.C.
October 2, 1975

The Beef Research and Information Act was a new bill up for consideration before the U.S. House of Representatives. It would enable cattle producers to conduct research and develop consumer information and markets for beef products. But Congressman Silvio Conte of Massachusetts thought it was not the best way to spend the taxpayers' money, and he "ribbed" his colleagues in the House about it.

☆ ☆

Mr. Chairman, I rise to assure my colleagues that I would not 'steer' them wrong, but I must 'raise a beef' about this bill.

This 'choice' legislation is a 'prime' example of what can make Congress 'stew in its own juices.'

It drips with excess 'fat,' while it 'strips' the consumer.

This 'beef-doggle' would raise retail meat prices by $60 million a year. No matter how you 'slice' it, consumers are having their 'flanks' attacked. They are being 'slaughtered.'

It was not my intent to 'roast' the sponsors of this 'bum steer.' But I must remind them that consumers have a 'stake' here too. But if this bill is 'herded' through the House, many consumers will no longer have 'steak.'

You have all heard of Britain's 'Rump Parliament' under Lord Cromwell. I fear that if this private interest bill for the beef industry passes, history will hereafter refer to us as the 'Rump-Roast Congress.'

I ask my colleagues to take this 'bull by the horns,' kill this bill, 'cut the fat off the bone,' and 'render' it back to the committee. It 'butchers' lean consumer pocketbooks, and makes 'mincemeat' of fiscal responsibility.

While I do not want to 'rib' my friends from the cattle-raising States, I think that someone is trying to 'pull the cowhide over our eyes.'

I urge my colleagues to reject this 'hunk of fat.' It bleeds the American consumer. And I do not know a 'knock wurst' than that.

Dr. Seuss

Commencement Address at Lake Forest College

Lake Forest, Illinois
June 4, 1977

Dr. Seuss was the pen name taken by beloved children's book author Theodor Seuss Geisel. His short commencement address to the graduating seniors of Lake Forest College, Illinois, included advice on cultivating a healthy skepticism, delivered in his familiar whimsical verse.

☆ ☆

"**M**y Uncle Terwilliger on the Art of Eating Popovers"

My uncle ordered popovers
from the restaurant's bill of fare,
and, when they were served, he regarded them
with a penetrating stare. . . .
Then he spoke great Words of Wisdom
as he sat there on that chair:
"To eat these things," said my uncle,
"You must exercise great care.
You may swallow down what's solid . . .
BUT . . . you must spit out the air!"

And . . . as you partake of the world's bill of fare,
that's darned good advice to follow.
Do a lot of spitting out the hot air.
And be careful what you swallow.

Esther Cohen

At the Liberators Conference

Washington, D.C.
October 27, 1981

Esther Cohen, born in Poland, lost most of her extended family in the Holocaust. She was liberated from Nazi persecution in 1945 and was only ten years old when she arrived at New York's immigration station on Ellis Island. In 1981, as a member of the U.S. Holocaust Memorial Council, she testified at the International Liberators Conference along with military personnel who had liberated the concentration camps. She spoke in answer to the question "How did you feel at liberation?"

☆ ☆

To speak of liberation and what it means to me is to speak from the heart and the soul, and probably for hours. . . .

At the actual time of liberation, I do not think I truly believed it was over. Certainly, hard as I tried, I could never begin to understand the madness, the blackness, and the brutality of the years past that were now over. What I did know was that for the first time in what seemed like an eternity, people had smiles on their faces, even if those smiles lasted only a moment, as their minds flashed back to those lost, to a world gone mad, to acts and events that were beyond human comprehension.

What I remember best is my father taking me in his arms and saying to me, "My dear child. Our family, once a strong beautiful tree, is no more. They have chopped it in pieces and cast those pieces in the inferno. But a branch has survived, and now that branch must grow, and from it must come new life." Those words and my mother's eyes when she looked at me have remained in my heart and my soul as a reminder that somehow I lived when so many others did not.

But it was some time later that I began to feel free and secure. It was in the United States, in New York, at our first apartment—a small room with two cots and a small bathroom down the hall shared with many families. It was and is to this day the best place I have ever lived in, for in that small room I could read, I could dream, I could do whatever my heart desired, and no one could come to harm me. I was free—free at last. I could go to school, walk the streets, I could go to the synagogue with my family on the Sabbath. I could even have friends with whom I could argue about different issues, and they would still be my friends. I could no longer be hurt because I was born a Jew.

As the years went on, the meaning of being free took on much deeper feelings. There was the inevitable question of "Why me? Why did I survive?" Eventually I gave up on that question, for I knew that I would never have the answer.

But yet, some answers did come to other questions. Yes, there were people out there who cared, who were willing to give their lives so that we could live and maybe, more importantly, so that mankind might have a just reason to go on. For as our brothers and sisters were dying, with them was vanishing any and all reason for the human race to continue.

It is today in this room that I feel the meaning of liberation. It is at the polling booths in my city when I am free to follow my conscience that I know the full meaning of my liberation. It is when I watch the sun rise in Jerusalem that I joyfully cry for being free.

I thank God, and I thank the men and women who fought so valiantly to free me and to restore justice and reason. I will never forget.

*Samantha Smith displays the letter she received from
Soviet Premier Yuri Andropov.*

Samantha Smith

"Look Around and See Only Friends"

Kobe, Japan
December 26, 1983

When ten-year-old Samantha Smith of Maine wrote to Soviet Premier Yuri Andropov of her worry over the potential for nuclear war between the United States and the Soviet Union, she received a personal letter and an invitation to visit. Her tour of the Soviet Union in the summer of 1983 endeared her to the Russian people. That fall, as a young spokesperson for peace, she was invited to address the Children's Symposium on the Year 2001 held in Kobe, Japan. Sadly, Samantha and her father were killed in a plane crash two years later.

☆ ☆

I have to begin with an apology. My father helped me with my speech, and look—I discovered that he doesn't know a single word of Japanese!

Luckily, I have learned some of your language. Since I got here, I've been trying to learn as much as possible. So let me begin by saying *Nihon no minasan Konnichiwa* [Hello everybody in Japan]. . . .

Until last April, I had never traveled outside the eastern United States. I had never even heard of sushi!

Then, because I had written a letter to Yuri Andropov, I found myself in Moscow, in Leningrad, and at a beautiful camp on the Black Sea near Yalta. I was on airplanes that took me over many foreign countries. After my trip to Russia—which actually should be called the Soviet Union—I came back to the same school and the same teachers and the same kids in Manchester, Maine. I didn't think I had changed at all, but, boy, had they changed! . . .

But today, we're not here to look back on the summer or to look backward at all. We're here to look ahead. I spent the last several weeks picturing myself in the year 2001, and thought of all the things that I would like the world to be eighteen years from today.

First of all, I don't want to have these freckles anymore, and I want this tooth straightened, and I hope I'll like the idea of being almost thirty. Maybe it's because I've traveled a lot and maybe it's because I've met so many wonderful people who look a little different from the way I look—maybe their skin, or their eyes, or their language is not like mine—but I can picture them becoming my best friends. . . . Maybe it's because of these things that I think the year 2001 and the years that follow are going to be just great. . . .

What I wish for is something I'll call the International Granddaughter Exchange. I guess if I were a boy, I'd call it the International Grandson Exchange. But, I'm not a boy, so I'll stick with granddaughter. The International Granddaughter Exchange would have the highest political leaders in nations all over the world sending their granddaughters or nieces—(or, okay, grandsons or nephews)—to live with families of opposite nations. Soviet leaders' granddaughters would spend two weeks in America. American leaders' granddaughters would spend two weeks in the Soviet Union. And, wherever possible, granddaughters of other opposing countries would exchange visits, and we would have better understanding all over the world.

And now I will say my wish in Japanese: *Sekaiju ni heiwa ga kimasu yo ni* [I wish for world peace and understanding].

Last summer, I had the amazing chance to visit the beautiful and awesome Soviet Union. I loved making friends with those girls and boys, and I think they enjoyed meeting an American kid. Let's keep doing it! Let's find a way to get some of those girls and boys to visit Japan, and America, and China, and Peru. And let's find a way for you to visit Soviet kids and American kids, kids who can't speak a word of Japanese—even kids who drive in American cars.

If we start with an International Granddaughter Exchange and keep expanding it and expanding it, then the year 2001 can be the year when all of us can look around and see only friends, no opposite nations, no enemies, and no bombs.

My grandparents are not important political leaders. In fact, one grandfather of mine was a doctor and one is a retired minister. But I've had the privilege of being an international granddaughter, and let me tell you that it is one terrific experience. . . .

My father, who is back in Maine, didn't help me with the end of my speech, so he'll probably be surprised when I say, Why don't you all come back home with me and meet my friends there!

Thank you for your attention. *Dōmo arigato gozai mashita!*

☆

Ronald Reagan

To the Nation on the Challenger Disaster

Washington, D.C.
January 28, 1986

Ronald Reagan, the president so celebrated for his speeches he was known as the "Great Communicator," was to deliver his yearly State of the Union message on the evening of January 28, 1986. That morning at the Kennedy Space Center in Florida, high school history teacher Christa McAuliffe joined six other astronauts on the shuttle Challenger. *Within minutes of lift-off,* Challenger *exploded and all aboard were killed. Horrified children in schools across the United States saw the disaster live on television; some schools even closed and sent children home. At the end of his speech to the nation that evening, President Reagan quoted from the poem "High Flight" by John Gillespie Magee, a young American flyer killed in World War II.*

☆ ☆

Ladies and gentlemen, I'd planned to speak to you tonight to report on the state of the Union, but the events of earlier today have led me to change those plans. Today is a day for mourning and remembering.

Nancy and I are pained to the core by the tragedy of the shuttle *Challenger*. We know we share this pain with all of the people of our country. This is truly a national loss.

Nineteen years ago, almost to the day, we lost three astronauts in a terrible accident on the ground. But we've never lost an astronaut in flight; we've never had a tragedy like this. And perhaps we've forgotten the courage it took for the crew of the shuttle; but they, the *Challenger* Seven, were aware of the dangers. . . . They had a hunger to explore the universe and discover its truths. They wished to serve, and they did. They served all of us.

We've grown used to wonders in this century. It's hard to dazzle us. But for twenty-five years the United States space program has been doing just that. We've grown used to the idea of space, and perhaps we forget that we've only just begun. We're still pioneers. They, the members of the *Challenger* crew, were pioneers.

And I want to say something to the schoolchildren of America who were watching the live coverage of the shuttle's takeoff. I know it is hard to understand, but sometimes painful things like this happen. It's all part of the process of exploration and discovery. It's all part of taking a chance and expanding man's horizons. The future doesn't belong to the fainthearted; it belongs to the brave. The *Challenger* crew was pulling us into the future, and we'll continue to follow them.

I've always had great faith in and respect for our space program, and what happened today does nothing to diminish it. We don't hide our space program. We don't keep secrets and cover things up. We do it all up front and in public. That's the way freedom is, and we wouldn't change it for a minute.

We'll continue our quest in space. There will be more shuttle flights and more shuttle crews and yes, more volunteers, more civilians, more teachers in space. Nothing ends here; our hopes and our journeys continue. . . .

On this day 390 years ago, the great explorer Sir Francis Drake died aboard ship off the coast of Panama. In his lifetime the great frontiers were the oceans, and a historian later said, "He lived by the sea, died on it, and was buried in it." Well, today we can say of the *Challenger* crew: Their dedication was, like Drake's, complete.

The crew of the space shuttle *Challenger* honored us by the manner in which they lived their lives. We will never forget them, nor the last time we saw them, this morning, as they prepared for their journey and waved good-bye and "slipped the surly bonds of earth" to "touch the face of God."

☆

Thurgood Marshall

On the Bicentennial of the Constitution

Maui, Hawaii
May 6, 1987

Thurgood Marshall was chief counsel for the National Association for the Advancement of Colored People for many years, and in 1964 he became the first black American appointed to the Supreme Court. During the year-long celebration of the 200th birthday of the Constitution, in 1987, Marshall gave a speech in Hawaii reflecting on the shortcomings of the original document.

☆ ☆

1987 marks the 200th anniversary of the United States Constitution. . . . Like many anniversary celebrations, . . . the tendency [is] for the celebration to oversimplify, and overlook the many other events that have been instrumental to our achievements as a nation. The focus of this celebration invites a complacent belief that the vision of those who debated and compromised in Philadelphia yielded the "more perfect Union" it is said we now enjoy. . . .

I do not believe that the meaning of the Constitution was forever "fixed" at the Philadelphia Convention. Nor do I find the wisdom, foresight, and sense of justice exhibited by the Framers particularly profound. To the contrary, the government they devised was defective from the start, requiring several amendments, a civil war, and momentous social transformation to attain the system of constitutional government, and its respect for the individual freedoms and human rights, we hold as fundamental today. . . .

For a sense of the evolving nature of the Constitution we need look no further than the first three words of the document's preamble: "We the People." When the Founding Fathers used this phrase in 1787, they did not have in mind the majority of America's citizens. "We the People" included, in the words of the Framers, "the whole Number of free Persons." On a matter so basic as the right to vote, for example, Negro slaves were excluded, although they were counted for representational purposes—at three-fifths each. Women did not gain the right to vote for over a hundred and thirty years.

These omissions were intentional. The record of the Framers' debates on the slave question is especially clear: The Southern States acceded to the demands of the New England States for giving Congress broad power to regulate commerce, in exchange for the right to continue the slave trade. . . . It took a bloody civil war before the 13th Amendment could be adopted to abolish slavery, though not the consequences slavery would have for future Americans.

While the Union survived the civil war, the Constitution did not. In its place arose a new, more promising basis for justice and equality, the 14th Amendment, ensuring protection of the life, liberty, and property of *all* persons against deprivations without due process, and guaranteeing equal protection of the laws. . . . Along the way, new constitutional principles have emerged to meet the challenges of a changing society. The progress has been dramatic, and it will continue.

The men who gathered in Philadelphia in 1787 could not have envisioned these changes. They could not have imagined, nor would they have accepted, that the document they were drafting would one day be construed by a Supreme Court to which had been appointed a woman and the descendent of an African slave. "We the People" no longer enslave, but the credit does not belong to the Framers. It belongs to those who refused to acquiesce in outdated notions of "liberty," "justice," and "equality," and who strived to better them.

And so we must be careful, when focusing on the events which took place in Philadelphia two centuries ago, that we not overlook the momentous events which followed, and thereby lose our proper sense of perspective. Otherwise, the odds are that for many Americans the bicentennial celebration will be little more than a blind pilgrimage to the shrine of the original document now stored in a vault in the National Archives. If we seek, instead, a sensitive understanding of the Constitution's inherent defects, and its promising evolution through 200 years of history, the celebration of the "Miracle at Philadelphia" will, in my view, be a far more meaningful and humbling experience. We will see that the true miracle was not the birth of the Constitution, but its life, a life nurtured through two turbulent centuries of our own making, and a life embodying much good fortune that was not [of our own making].

Thus in this bicentennial year, we may not all participate in the festivities with flag-waving fervor. Some may more quietly commemorate the suffering, struggle, and sacrifice that has triumphed over much of what was wrong with the original document, and observe the anniversary with hopes not realized and promises not fulfilled. I plan to celebrate the bicentennial of the Constitution as a living document, including the Bill of Rights and the other amendments protecting individual freedoms and human rights.

President Ronald Reagan at the Brandenburg Gate.

Ronald Reagan

"Mr. Gorbachev, Tear Down This Wall!"

Berlin, then West Germany
June 12, 1987

In 1987, with the Cold War still in force, President Ronald Reagan stood at Berlin's Brandenburg Gate and challenged Soviet leader Mikhail Gorbachev to demolish the Berlin Wall separating East Berlin from West Berlin. Erected in 1961 by the Soviets to keep East Germans from fleeing to the West, the Wall was finally dismantled in 1989.

☆ ☆

Twenty-four years ago, President John F. Kennedy visited Berlin, speaking to the people of this city and the world at the City Hall. Well, since then two other presidents have come, each in his turn, to Berlin. And today I, myself, make my second visit to your city. We come to Berlin, we American presidents, because it's our duty to speak, in this place, of freedom. . . .

271

Behind me stands a wall that encircles the free sectors of this city, part of a vast system of barriers that divides the entire continent of Europe. From the Baltic, south, those barriers cut across Germany in a gash of barbed wire, concrete, dog runs, and guard towers. . . .Yet it is here in Berlin where the wall emerges most clearly; here, cutting across your city, where the news photo and the television screen have imprinted this brutal division of a continent upon the mind of the world. Standing before the Brandenburg Gate, every man is a German, separated from his fellow men. Every man is a Berliner, forced to look upon a scar.

President von Weizsäcker has said, "The German question is open as long as the Brandenburg Gate is closed." Today I say: As long as this gate is closed, as long as this scar of a wall is permitted to stand, it is not the German question alone that remains open, but the question of freedom for all mankind. Yet I do not come here to lament. For I find in Berlin a message of hope, even in the shadow of this wall, a message of triumph. . . .

In the 1950s, Khruschev predicted: "We will bury you." But in the West today, we see a free world that has achieved a level of prosperity and well-being unprecedented in all human history. In the Communist world, we see failure, technological backwardness, declining standards of health, even want of the most basic kind—too little food. Even today, the Soviet Union still cannot feed itself. After these four decades, then, there stands before the entire world one great and inescapable conclusion: Freedom leads to prosperity. Freedom replaces the ancient hatreds among the nations with comity and peace. Freedom is the victor.

And now the Soviets themselves may, in a limited way, be coming to understand the importance of freedom. We hear much from Moscow about a new policy of reform and openness. Some political prisoners have been released. Certain foreign news broadcasts are no longer being jammed. Some economic enterprises have been permitted to operate with greater freedom from state control. Are these the beginnings of profound changes in the Soviet State? Or are they token gestures, intended to raise false hopes in the West? . . . We welcome change and openness, for we believe that freedom and security go together, that the advance of human liberty can only strengthen the cause of world peace.

There is one sign the Soviets can make that would be unmistakable, that would advance dramatically the cause of freedom and peace.

General Secretary Gorbachev, if you seek peace, if you seek prosperity for the Soviet Union and Eastern Europe, if you seek liberalization: Come here to this gate! Mr. Gorbachev, open this gate! Mr. Gorbachev, tear down this wall!

I understand the fear of war and the pain of division that afflict this continent—and I pledge to you my country's efforts to help overcome these burdens. To be sure, we in the West must resist Soviet expansion. So we must maintain defenses of unassailable strength. Yet we seek peace; so we must strive to reduce arms on both sides. . . . Today we have within reach the possibility, not merely of limiting the growth of arms, but of eliminating, for the first time, an entire class of nuclear weapons from the face of the earth. . . .

But we must remember a crucial fact: East and West do not mistrust each other because we are armed; we are armed because we mistrust each other. And our differences are not about weapons but about liberty. When President Kennedy spoke at the City Hall those twenty-four years ago, freedom was encircled, Berlin was under siege. And today, despite all the pressures upon this city, Berlin stands secure in its liberty. And freedom itself is transforming the globe. . . .

As I looked out a moment ago from the Reichstag, that embodiment of German unity, I noticed words crudely spray-painted upon the wall, perhaps by a young Berliner: "This wall will fall. Beliefs become reality." Yes, across Europe, this wall will fall. For it cannot withstand faith; it cannot withstand truth. The wall cannot withstand freedom.

☆

Jesse Jackson

To the Democratic National Convention

Atlanta, Georgia
July 20, 1988

A civil rights activist and Baptist minister who marched with Martin Luther King, Reverend Jesse Jackson twice ran for president of the United States, the first African American to do so. In 1988, he addressed the Democratic National Convention in Atlanta, Georgia. Hoping the next day to receive the party's nomination for president, he shared his personal story at the close of his speech.

☆ ☆

I have a story. I wasn't always on television. Writers were not always outside my door. When I was born late one afternoon, October 8th, in Greenville, South Carolina, no writers asked my mother her name. Nobody chose to write down our address. My mama was not supposed to make it. And I was not supposed to make it. You see, I was born to a teen-age mother who was born to a teen-age mother.

I understand. I know abandonment and people being mean to you, and saying you're nothing and nobody, and can never be anything. I understand. Jesse Jackson is my third name. I'm adopted. When I had no name, my grandmother gave me her name. My name was Jesse Burns until I was twelve. So I wouldn't have a blank space, she gave me a name to hold me over. I understand when nobody knows your name. I understand when you have no name. I understand.

I wasn't born in the hospital. Mama didn't have insurance. I was born in the bed at home. I really do understand. Born in a three-room-house, bathroom in the backyard, slop jar by the bed, no hot and cold running water. I understand. Wallpaper used for decoration? No. For a windbreaker. I understand.

I'm a working person's person, that's why I understand you whether you're black or white.

I understand work. I was not born with a silver spoon in my mouth. I had a shovel programmed for my hand. My mother, a working woman. So many days she went to work early with runs in her stockings. She knew better, but she wore runs in her stockings so that my brother and I could have matching socks and not be laughed at at school.

I understand. At 3 o'clock on Thanksgiving Day we couldn't eat turkey because mama was preparing someone else's turkey at 3 o'clock. We had to play football to entertain ourselves and then around 6 o'clock she would get off the Alta Vista bus; then we would bring up the leftovers and eat our turkey—leftovers, the carcass, the cranberries around 8 o'clock at night. I really do understand.

Every one of these funny labels they put on you, those of you who are watching this broadcast tonight in the projects, on the corners, I understand. Call you outcast, low down, you can't make it, you're nothing, you're from nobody, subclass, underclass—when you see Jesse Jackson, when my name goes in nomination, your name goes in nomination.

I was born in the slum, but the slum was not born in me. And it wasn't born in you, and you can make it. Wherever you are tonight you can make it. Hold your head high, stick your chest out. You can make it. It gets dark sometimes, but the morning comes. Don't you surrender. Suffering breeds character. Character breeds faith. In the end faith will not disappoint.

You must not surrender. You may or may not get there, but just know that you're qualified and you hold on and hold out. We must never surrender. America will get better and better. Keep hope alive. Keep hope alive. Keep hope alive. On tomorrow night and beyond, keep hope alive.

I love you very much. I love you very much.

Daniel Inouye

To the 442nd Infantry
Regimental Combat Team

Honolulu, Hawaii
March 24, 1993

After Japan bombed Pearl Harbor, on December 7, 1941, thousands of Japanese Americans were unfairly imprisoned in camps by the U.S. government under suspicion of being enemy aliens. Daniel Inouye of Hawaii joined the army in 1943 and lost an arm to a German grenade in Italy. He became the first U.S. congressman from the new state of Hawaii, and the first of Japanese descent, in 1959. Senator Inouye returned to Honolulu in 1993 to address the 50th reunion of his decorated World War II regiment of Japanese American soldiers.

☆ ☆

Although this is our 50th reunion, our journey began . . . on December 7, 1941 [at Pearl Harbor, Hawaii].

Soon after that tragic Sunday morning, we who were of Japanese ancestry were considered by our nation to be citizens without a country. I am certain all of us remember that the Selective Service system of our country designated us to be unfit for military service because we were "enemy aliens." Soon after that, on February 19, 1942, the White House issued an extraordinary Executive Order—Executive Order 9066. This dreaded Executive Order forcibly uprooted our mainland brothers and their families and their loved ones from their homes with only those possessions that they were able to carry themselves. . . .

Their only crime, if any, was that they were born of Japanese parents, and for that crime they were incarcerated in internment camps surrounded by barbed-wire fences, guarded by machine-gun towers. . . .

Although we were separated by a vast ocean and mountain ranges, we from the mainland and Hawaii shared one deep-seated desire—to rid ourselves of that insulting and degrading designation, "enemy alien." We wanted to serve our country. We wanted to demonstrate our love for our country.

After many months of petitions and letters, another Executive Order was issued with the declaration that ". . .Americanism is a matter of mind and heart; Americanism is not, and never was, a matter of race or ancestry." By this Executive Order, the formation of the special combat team made up of Japanese Americans was authorized.

More than the anticipated numbers volunteered; in fact, in Hawaii, about eighty-five percent of the eligible men of Japanese Americans volunteered. . . . We were ready to live up to our motto, "Go for Broke." And thus the 442nd Infantry Regimental Combat Team was formed.

There are too many battles to recall. . . . But there is one we will never forget and one hopefully that our nation will always remember—the Battle of the Lost Battalion.

This battle began during the last week of October 1944. The members of the First Battalion of the 141st Infantry Regiment of the 36th Texas Division found themselves surrounded by a large number of enemy troops. This "lost battalion" was ordered to fight its way back, but could not do so. The Second and Third Battalions of the Texas Regiment were ordered to break through but they were thrown back, and so on October 26, the 442nd was ordered to go into the lines to rescue the "lost battalion." On November 15, the rescue was successfully concluded. . . .

Two thousand men were in hospitals and over three hundred had died. The price was heavy. Although we did not whimper or complain, we were sensitive to the fact that the rescuers of the Texas Battalion were not members of the Texas Division. They were Japanese Americans from Hawaii and from mainland internment camps. They were "enemy aliens." . . .

And we knew that from that moment on, no one could ever, ever, question our loyalty and our love for our country. The insulting stigma was finally taken away. . . .

Over the years, many have asked us—"Why?" "Why did you fight and serve so well?" My son, like your sons and daughters, has asked the same question—"Why?" "Why were you willing and ready to give your life?" . . .

I told my son it was a matter of honor. I told him about my father's farewell message when I left home to put on the uniform of my country. My father was not a man of eloquence but he said, "Whatever you do, do not dishonor the family and do not dishonor the country." I told my son that for many of us, to have done any less than what we had done in battle would have dishonored our families and our country.

Second, I told my son that there is an often-used Japanese phrase—*Kodomo no tame ni* [for the children]. Though most of us who went into battle were young and single, we wanted to leave a legacy of honor and pride and the promise of a good life for our yet-to-be-born children and their children.

My brothers, I believe we can assure ourselves that we did succeed in upholding our honor and that of our families and our nation. And I respectfully and humbly believe that our service and the sacrifices of those who gave their all on the battlefield assure a better life for our children and their children.

☆

Cal Ripken Jr.

To His Fans

Baltimore, Maryland
September 6, 1995

"Iron Man" Cal Ripken Jr., shortstop for the Baltimore Orioles baseball team, broke "Iron Horse" Lou Gehrig's longstanding record for most consecutive games played in 1995 at the Orioles' home park of Camden Yards. Ripken received an ovation lasting over ten minutes when the game was official after the fifth inning, and he addressed the adoring crowd at a post-game ceremony.

☆ ☆

Tonight, I want to make sure you know how I feel. As I grew up here, I not only had dreams of being a big-league ballplayer, but also of being a Baltimore Oriole. As a boy and a fan, I know how passionate we feel about baseball and the Orioles here. And as a player, I have benefitted from this passion.

For all of your support over the years, I want to thank you, the fans of Baltimore, from the bottom of my heart. This is the greatest place to play.

This year has been unbelievable. I've been cheered in ball-parks all over the country. People not only showed me their kindness, but more importantly, they demonstrated their love of the game of baseball. I give my thanks to baseball fans everywhere. . . .

Tonight, I stand here, overwhelmed, as my name is linked with the great and courageous Lou Gehrig. I'm truly humbled to have our names spoken in the same breath.

Some may think our greatest connection is because we both played many consecutive games. Yet, I believe in my heart that our true link is a common motivation—a love of the game of baseball, a passion for our team, and a desire to compete on the very highest level.

I know that if Lou Gehrig is looking on tonight's activities, he isn't concerned about someone playing one more consecutive game than he did. Instead, he's viewing tonight as just another example of what is good and right about the great American game. Whether your name is Gehrig or Ripken, DiMaggio, or Robinson, or that of some youngster who picks up his bat or puts on his glove, you are challenged by the game of baseball to do your very best day in and day out. And that's all I've tried to do.

Charles S. Robb

"They Died for That Which Can Never Burn"

U.S. Senate, Washington, D.C.
March 28, 2000

Senator Charles Robb of Virginia served in the Marine Corps in Vietnam as commander of an infantry company in combat. He returned in 1969 to find the United States in turmoil over the war. His next assignment was to recruit officers for the Marines from college campuses, a job which put him into the thick of antiwar demonstrations where the American flag was occasionally burned to protest government support for the war. When an amendment to the Constitution was proposed in 1999 to punish flag burners, Robb offered his thoughts as one who had seen the flag both revered and reviled.

☆ ☆

Mr. President, I am repulsed by any individual who would burn the flag of my country to convey a message of dissent. It is an act I abhor and can barely comprehend. But in the democracy that our forefathers founded, and that generations of Americans have fought and died to preserve, I simply do not have the right to decide how another individual expresses his or her political views. I can abhor those political views, but I cannot imprison someone for expressing them. That's a fundamental tenet of democracies and it's what makes America the envy of the world, as the home of the free and the brave. . . .

Last week, I received an e-mail from a retired United States Marine Corps Colonel who happened to be from Virginia. Like many Americans, and many American veterans, he had struggled with this issue and searched his conscience for what's right. In his message to me, he said: "I have seen our flag torn in battle, captured by our enemies, and trampled on by protesters. In all those events I never felt that the American way of life was in grave peril . . . for whenever our flag fell or was destroyed there was always another Marine to step forward and pull a replacement from his helmet or ruck sack."

He continued: "The Constitution is the bedrock of America, the nation . . . the people. It is not possible to pull another such document from our 'national ruck sack.' We have but one Constitution, and it should be the object of our protection."

Mr. President, there is no question that it is precisely *because* the flag represents those sacred ideals that define our democracy, that we are so angry to see one being trampled or torn or torched. . . .

In fact, Mr. President, it is the *motivation* of the flag burner, not the burning of the flag itself, that makes us so angry that we want to punish that individual and throw away the keys. We know that when an American flag is old and tattered, or damaged and no longer fit to fly, we don't bury it, or throw it in the trash. We burn it. That is the proper, respectful method of disposing of a flag. So it is not the *burning* of the flag that stirs us to anger. It is the *reason* why the flag was burned that gets us so upset. And the reason why the flag is burned—to convey a message of dissent—is the reason why the Constitution protects it. . . .

Mr. President, I *am* a proud veteran of the United States Marine Corps. And I learned many lessons serving in Vietnam. I served with Marines who loved this country and were great patriots. They were often young and sometimes scared. But they risked their lives in Southeast Asia.

Some of those brave warriors died for our nation. On two separate occasions, I had men literally die in my arms. Those who made the ultimate sacrifice may have died keeping faith with their country. They may have died so that others might be free. They may have died for an ideal or a principle or a promise—sacred intangibles that transcend time. Some might say they died for the flag. But I was there, Mr. President, and they did not die for a piece of cloth, however sacred, that eventually becomes worn and tattered and eventually has to be replaced. No. They died fighting for all that our flag represents.

My fellow veterans who died in combat sacrificed their lives for these intangibles that are the core values of our democracy. They died for liberty and tolerance, for justice and equality. They died for that which can never burn. They died for ideals that can only be desecrated by our failure to defend them.

And in opposing this amendment, Mr. President, I truly believe that I am again called upon to defend those intangible ideals—like freedom and tolerance—for which so many of us fought, and too many of us died. I am in a different uniform today, in a different place and time. But I feel as if, in some way, I am again battling the odds to defend principles that, as a younger man, I was willing to die for. I'd still put my life on the line today to defend those same principles.

I say that, Mr. President, because the flag *represents* freedom to me. But the First Amendment *guarantees* that freedom. And when we seek to punish those who express views we don't share, then *we*—not the flag burners—*we* begin to erode the very values, the very freedoms, that make America the greatest democracy the world has ever known.

Appendix
To the Young Speaker

Public speaking is as valuable a talent today as it was for the Romans two thousand years ago, and a skill anyone can learn. If you've ever given a book report, or asked members of your class to vote for you, you've already engaged in public speaking. When you practice public speaking by delivering a speech given before by someone else, it's called *declamation*, a method used for hundreds of years for studying *oratory*, the making of speeches. When you give the speech, you are *declaiming*. In a similar fashion, artists sometimes copy great paintings as a way of discovering the techniques of a great master's art.

Choose a speech that inspires you, or a speaker you admire. It's important to practice the speech several times, to make sure you can pronounce all the words and know what the speech is saying. Ask someone about, or look up in a book, any references in the speech that are unfamiliar. It's difficult to make the words sound like your own if you don't understand what they mean. Find out what you can about the background of the speech and the speaker, and put the feeling into your voice that you imagine the original speaker might have had. Practice out loud, in front of family or friends (or even a mirror), resisting the temptation to speak too quickly.

When the time comes to make your speech, remember that your audience is your friend—they want you to do well, and they look forward to what you're going to say. They won't be at all as critical of your performance as you are of yourself. Smile at the audience when you first stand up in front, and see how you relax when they smile back. Don't begin until they are ready to listen—look around the room and get their attention.

Give an introduction to your speech with several sentences in your own words that tell your listeners who gave the speech originally and to what sort of audience, when and where it occurred, and why it was given. This will increase their enjoyment and understanding enormously. Be kind to your audience by speaking slowly, and pausing occasionally—remember, you are more familiar with the speech than they are. Rushing through the speech leaves the audience racing to follow the ideas you're presenting, and if they lose the point of what you're saying, you may lose their attention; Mark Twain depended enormously for his success as a speaker on his superbly timed pauses. Make eye contact with your audience as often as you can. Speak louder sometimes, for emphasis.

When you're finished, you can thank your audience, and pause a moment while you accept their applause.

If you enjoyed declaiming, you may want to join a debate group at your school to continue the experience, and even write your own speeches and participate in debates. Many great statesmen or stateswomen, Barbara Jordan for instance, were members of their school "forensic" teams. Remember what Russell Conwell said—if you would be an orator as a man or woman, you must speak your piece as a boy or girl.

Permissions

Photo Credits

Page 25, National Archives

Page 46, *Black Hawk* by George Caitlin, National Museum of American Art, Washington, D.C./ Art Resource, NY

Page 49, National Archives

Page 64, Courtesy of the American Antiquarian Society

Page 69, Courtesy of the Massachusetts Historical Society

Page 91, National Archives

Page 104, Courtesy of the Washington State Historical Society, Tacoma

Page 109, © Bettmann/CORBIS

Page 117, Courtesy of the Newberry Library, Chicago

Page 143, © Bettmann/CORBIS

Page 149, AP/Wide World Photos

Page 158, © Bettmann/CORBIS

Page 167, National Archives

Page 169, AP/Wide World Photos

Page 171, National Archives, U.S. Army photo

Page 176, National Archives and Records Administration, courtesy AIP Emilio Segre Visual Archives

Page 190, Courtesy of the Richard Nixon Library and Birthplace

Page 200, Frank Scherschel/Timepix

Page 208, Photographs and Prints Division, Schomburg Center for Research in Black Culture, The New York Public Library

Page 220, Courtesy of the Arizona Historical Foundation, Arizona State University, Tempe, Arizona

Page 234, Walter P. Reuther Library, Wayne State University

Page 242, Glinn/Magnum Photos

Page 263, © Bettmann/CORBIS

Page 271, Courtesy Ronald Reagan Library

Index of Speakers

Index of Themes

abolition. *See* slavery
Alamo, 49
animals, 97, 169, 190
arms control, 176, 200, 271
Army, U.S., 167, 171, 204, 276
atomic bomb, 176, 182. *See also*
    nuclear weapons

baseball, 158, 279
Berlin, 206, 271
black nationalism, 216

campaign speeches, 81, 83, 109,
    153, 169, 187, 190, 220, 274
child labor, 116, 117, 120, 127, 146
child poverty, 146, 225, 274
children, 106
    and school, 12, 184, 197, 266,
    and war, 104, 149
    and crime, 149
    and pets, 190
    and prejudice, 194, 197, 208,
    211, 225, 261,
    speeches by, 116, 263
civil rights, 95, 187, 192, 194, 208,
    211, 216, 223, 225, 239, 268
Civil War, 67, 89, 91, 93, 112, 268
communism, 179, 184, 197, 206,
    220, 271
Compromise of 1850, 67, 73
Constitution, U.S., 25, 28, 81, 83,
    101, 179, 253, 268, 281

democracy, 101, 140, 143, 173,
    184, 192, 197, 225, 281. *See*
    also republic
Depression, 155
draft, military, 143, 231, 236

eulogies, 87, 91, 97, 173, 214, 242.
    See also tributes

facism, 179, 184
flag, 281
foreign relations, 31, 34, 61, 176,
    197, 200, 206, 220, 229, 236,
    263, 271
freedom, 34, 43, 135, 160, 165,
    173, 268
    from British, 14, 17, 22
    from slavery, 56, 58, 64, 73, 87
    from prejudice, 184, 208, 216,
    261
    from oppression, 39, 171, 184,
    200, 206, 220, 271
freedom of the press, 9, 34, 51, 87
freedom of speech, 87, 143, 179,
    184, 223, 251, 281
friendship, 20, 263

government, 9, 31, 34, 43, 81.
    See also Constitution, U.S.;
    democracy
greatness, 112, 133

Holocaust, 261
humor, 122, 169, 258, 260

immigration, 135, 261
inaugural, 34, 93, 155, 200

Japanese-American, 276

labor, 109, 116, 117, 120, 127, 146,
    155, 234
land, 36, 39, 46, 61, 76, 99, 104,
    248